A
MEDITATIVE
COMMENTARY
ON THE
NEW TESTAMENT

# ACTS OF THE APOSTLES
# JESUS ALIVE IN HIS CHURCH

by Earl Lavender

LEAFWOOD
PUBLISHERS

ACTS OF THE APOSTLES: JESUS ALIVE IN HIS CHURCH

Copyright 2006 by Earl Lavender

ISBN 978-0-89112-501-3

Printed in the United States of America

Cover design by Thinkpen Design, LLC

For information contact:
Leafwood Publishers, Abilene, Texas
1-877-816-4455 toll free
www.leafwoodpublishers.com

12 13 14 15 16 17 / 7 6 5 4 3 2

*To Mark and Martha,*
*in prayerful thanksgiving for your passionate hearts*
*in continual support of kingdom missions*

## Acknowledgements

I am deeply thankful to Gary Holloway for his writing and editing. His work in this series is wonderful. I am also thankful to Leonard Allen, my editor at Leafwood Publishers, for his excitement and support for this effort. I would be remiss not to mention my thankfulness and love for the Donelson Church, who first asked me to develop these studies (Luke and Acts) for their use. I would also like to offer a special word of thanks to the "early birds," precious saints at the Woodmont Hills Family of God who have so diligently studied the word of God with me every Sunday morning at 7 a.m. for many years. And, of course, as always, none of this work could be done without the loving support of Rebecca, my wife. More than anyone else in my life, she has taught me the truth of God's word by living it.

# C O N T E N T S

## INTRODUCTION

## MEDITATIONS ON ACTS

# INTRODUCTION

# HEARING GOD IN SCRIPTURE

There are many commentaries, guides, and workbooks on the various books of the Bible. How is this series different? It is not intended to answer all your scholarly questions about the Bible, or even make you an expert in the details of Scripture. Instead, this series is designed to help you hear the voice of God for your everyday life. It is a guide to meditation on the Bible, meditation that will allow the Bible to transform you.

We read in many ways. We might scan the newspaper for information, read a map for location, read a novel for pleasure, or read a textbook to pass a test. These are all good ways to read, depending on our circumstances.

A young soldier far away from home who receives a letter from his wife reads in yet another way. He might scan the letter quickly at first for news and information. But his longing for his beloved causes him to read the letter again and again, hearing her sweet voice in every line. He slowly treasures each word of this precious letter.

## BIBLE STUDY

So also, there are many good ways to read the Bible, depending on our circumstances. Bible study is absolutely necessary for our life with God. We rightly study the Bible for information. We ask, "Who wrote this?" "When was it written?" "Who were the original readers?" "How do these words apply to me?" More importantly, we want information about God. Who is he? What does he think of me? What does he want from me?

There is no substitute for this kind of close, dedicated Bible study. We must know what the Bible says to know our standing with God. We therefore read the Bible to discover true doctrine or teaching. But some in their emphasis on the authority and inspiration of the Bible have forgotten that Bible study is not an end in itself. We want to know God through Scripture. We want to have a relationship with the Teacher, not just the teachings.

Jesus tells some of God's people in his day, "You diligently study the Scriptures because you think that by them you possess eternal life. These are the Scriptures that testify about me, yet you refuse to come to me to have life" (John 5:39-40). He's not telling them to study their Bibles less, but he is reminding them of the deeper purpose of Bible study—to draw us to God through Jesus. Bible study is a means, not an end.

Yet the way many of us have learned to study the Bible may actually get in the way of hearing God. "Bible study" may sound a lot like schoolwork, and many of us were happy to get out of school. "Bible study" may call to mind pictures of intellectuals surrounded by books in Greek and Hebrew, pondering meanings too deep for ordinary people. The method of Bible study that has been popular for some time focuses on the strangeness of the Bible. It was written long ago, far away, and in languages we cannot read. There is a huge gap between us and the original readers of the Bible, a gap that can only be bridged by scholars, not by average folk.

There is some truth and some value in that "scholarly" method. It is true that the Bible was not written originally to us. Knowing ancient languages and customs can at times help us understand the Bible better. However, one unintended result of this approach is to make

8

the Bible distant from the people of God. We may come to think that we can only hear God indirectly through Scripture, that his word must be filtered through scholars. We may even think that deep Bible study is a matter of mastering obscure information about the Bible.

## MEDITATION

But we read the Bible for more than information. By studying it, we experience transformation, the mysterious process of God at work in us. Through his loving words, God is calling us to life with him. He is forming us into the image of his Son.

Reading the Bible is not like reading other books. We are not simply trying to learn information or master material. Instead, we want to stand under the authority of Scripture and let God master us. While we read the Bible, it reads us, opening the depths of our being to the overpowering love of God. "For the word of God is living and active. Sharper than any double-edged sword, it penetrates even to dividing soul and spirit, joints and marrow; it judges the thoughts and attitudes of the heart. Nothing in all creation is hidden from God's sight. Everything is uncovered and laid bare before the eyes of him to whom we must give account" (Hebrews 4:12-13).

Opening our hearts to the word of God is meditation. Although this way of reading the Bible may be new to some, it has a long heritage among God's people. The Psalmist joyously meditates on the words of God (Psalm 1:2; 39:3; 119:15, 23, 27, 48, 78, 97, 99, 148). Meditation is taking the words of Scripture to heart and letting them ask questions of us. It is slowing chewing over a text, listening closely, reading God's message of love to us over and over. This is not a simple, easy, or naïve reading of Scripture, but a process that takes time, dedication, and practice on our part.

There are many ways to meditate on the Bible. One is praying the

Scriptures. Prayer and Bible study really cannot be separated. One way of praying the Bible is to make the words of a text your prayer. Obviously, the prayer texts of Scripture, especially the Psalms, lend themselves to this. "The Lord is my shepherd" has been the prayer of many hearts.

However, it is proper and helpful to turn the words of the Bible into prayers. Commands from God can become prayers. "You shall have no other gods before me" (Exodus 20:3) can be prayed, "Lord, keep me from anything that takes your place in my heart." Stories can be prayed. Jesus heals a man born blind (John 9), and so we pray, "Lord Jesus open my eyes to who you truly are." Even the promises of the Bible become prayers. "Never will I leave you; never will I forsake you" (Deuteronomy 31:6; Hebrews 13:5) becomes "God help me know that you promise that you are always with me and so live my life without fear."

Obviously, there are many helpful ways of hearing the voice of God in Scripture. Again, the purpose of Bible reading and study is not to know more about the Bible, much less to pride ourselves as experts on Scripture. Instead, we read to hear the voice of our Beloved. We listen for a word of God for us.

## HOLY READING

This commentary reflects one ancient way of meditation and praying the Scriptures known as *lectio divina* or holy reading. This method assumes that God wants to speak to us directly in the Bible, that the passage we are reading is God's word to us right now. The writers of the New Testament read the Old Testament with this same conviction. They saw the words of the Bible speaking directly to their own situation. They read with humility and with prayer.

The first step along this way of holy reading is listening to the

Bible. Choose a biblical text that is not too long. This commentary breaks Acts into smaller sections. The purpose is to hear God's voice in your current situation, not to cover material or prepare lessons. Get into a comfortable position and maintain silence before God for several minutes. This prepares the heart to listen. Read slowly. Savor each word. Perhaps read aloud. Listen for a particular phrase that speaks to you. Ask God, "What are you trying to tell me today?"

The next step is to meditate on that particular phrase. That meditation may include slowly repeating the phrase that seems to be for you today. As you think deeply on it, you might even memorize it. Committing biblical passages to memory allows us to hold them in our hearts all day long. If you keep a journal, you might write the passage there. Let those words sink deeply into your heart.

Then pray those words back to God in your heart. Those words may call up visual images, smells, sounds, and feelings. Pay attention to what God is giving you in those words. Then respond in faith to what those words say to your heart. What do they call you to be and to do? Our humble response might take the form of praise, thanksgiving, joy, confession, or even cries of pain.

The final step in this "holy reading" is contemplation of God. The words from God that we receive deeply in our hearts lead us to him. Through these words, we experience union with the all-powerful God of love. Again, one should not separate Bible reading from prayer. The words of God in Scripture transport us into the very presence of God where we joyfully rest in his love.

What keeps reading the Bible this way from becoming merely our own desires read back into Scripture? How do we know it is God's voice we hear and not our own?

Two things. One is prayer. We are asking God to open our hearts, minds, and lives to him. We ask to hear his voice, not ours and not the voice of the world around us.

The second thing that keeps this from being an exercise in self-deception is to study the Bible in community. By praying over Scripture in a group, we hear God's word together. God speaks through the other members of our group. The wisdom he gives them keeps us from private, selfish, and unusual interpretations. They help us keep our own voices in check, as we desire to listen to God alone.

## HOW TO USE THIS COMMENTARY

This commentary provides assistance in holy reading of the Bible. It gives structure to daily personal devotions, family meditation, small group Bible studies, and church classes.

### DAILY DEVOTIONAL

Listening, meditation, prayer, contemplation. How does this commentary fit into this way of Bible study? Consider it as a conversation partner. We have taken a section of Scripture and then broken it down into four short daily readings. After listening, meditating, praying, and contemplating the passage for the day, use the questions suggested in the commentary to provoke deeper reflection. This provides a structure for a daily fifteen minute devotional four days a week. On the fifth day, read the entire passage, meditate, and then use the questions to reflect on the meaning of the whole. On day six, take our meditations on the passage as conversation with another who has prayed over the text.

If you want to begin daily Bible reading, but need guidance, this provides a Monday–Saturday experience that prepares the heart for worship and praise on Sunday. This structure also results in a communal reading of Scripture, instead of a private reading. Even if you use this commentary alone, you are not reading privately. God is at work in you and in the conversation you have with another (the author of the commentary) who has sought to hear God through this particular passage of the Bible.

## FAMILY BIBLE STUDY

This commentary can also provide an arrangement for family Bible study. Many Christian parents want to lead their children in daily study, but don't know where to begin or how to structure their time. Using the six-day plan outlined above means the entire family can read, meditate, pray, and reflect on the shorter passages, using the questions provided. On day five, they can review the entire passage, and then on day six, read the meditations in the commentary to prompt reflection and discussion. God will bless our families beyond our imaginations through the prayerful study of his word.

## WEEKLY GROUP STUDY

This commentary can also structure small group Bible study. Each member of the group should have meditated over the daily readings and questions for the five days preceding the group meeting, using the method outlined above. The day before the group meeting, each member should read and reflect on the meditations in the commentary on that passage. You then can meet once a week to hear God's word together. In that group meeting, the method of holy reading would look something like this:

*Listening*
   1) Five minutes of silence.
   2) Slow reading of the biblical passage for that week.
   3) A minute of silent meditation on the passage.

4) Briefly share with the group the word or phrase that struck you.

*Personal Message*

5) A second reading of the same passage.

6) A minute of silence.

7) Where does this touch your life today?

8) Responses: I hear, I see, etc.

*Life Response*

9) Brief silence.

10) What does God want you to do today in light of this word?

*Group Prayer*

11) Have each member of the group pray aloud for the person on his or her left, asking God to bless the word he has given them.

The procedure suggested here can be used in churches or in neighborhood Bible studies. Church members would use the daily readings Monday–Friday in their daily devotionals. This commentary intentionally provides no readings on the sixth day, so that we can spend Saturdays as a time of rest, not rest from Bible study, but a time to let God's word quietly work its way deep into our hearts. Sunday during Bible school or in home meetings, the group would meet to experience the weekly readings together, using the group method described above. It might be that the sermon for each Sunday could be on the passage for that week.

There are churches that have used this structure to great advantage. In the hallways of those church buildings, the talk is not of the local football team or the weather, but of the shared experience of the Word of God for that week.

And that is the purpose of our personal and communal study, to hear the voice of God, our loving Father who wants us to love him in return. He deeply desires a personal relationship with us. Father, Son, and Spirit make a home inside us (see John 14:16-17, 23). Our loving God speaks to his children! But we must listen for his voice. That listening is not a matter of gritting our teeth and trying harder to hear. Instead, it is part of our entire life with God. That is what Bible study is all about.

Through daily personal prayer and meditation on God's word and through a communal reading of Scripture, our most important conversation partner, the Holy Spirit, will do his mysterious and marvelous work. Among other things, the Spirit pours God's love into our hearts (Romans 5:5), bears witness to our spirits that we are God's children (Romans 8:16), intercedes for us with God (Romans 8:26), and enlightens us as to God's will (Ephesians 1:17).

So this is an invitation to personal daily Bible study, to praying the Scriptures, to sharing with fellow believers, to hear the voice of God. God will bless us, our families, our churches, and his world if we take the time to be still, listen, and do his word.

# THE SPIRITUALITY OF ACTS

Acts is part two of Luke's Gospel. It is the story of how the church continued the embodiment of God's eternal purposes first incarnated by Jesus. The theme of Luke/Acts is God fulfilling his eternal purposes through Jesus, his Son, and then through Jesus' disciples—the church. The story of conversion does not end with one accepting Jesus as Lord. God has a purpose for what he accomplishes through salvation—and that is to reconcile us to him and return us to "the Way" for which he created us. Jesus perfectly embodies the life for which God created us. What Jesus does in Luke's account of the gospel, the church continues to do in Acts, thus continuing the fulfillment of God's will for life.

Luke-Acts is the telling of an exciting adventure of faithful obedience, first by the Son of God, who opens the way for his followers to live in that same obedience as they expand his mission into the world.

## BUILDING CONFIDENT FAITH
## IN JESUS AS THE CHRIST

Luke addresses both Luke and Acts to Theophilus. Whoever Theophilus might have been (see other commentaries for a number of ideas), for our purpose it is enough to recognize that Luke wanted to build his confidence that all he had heard about Jesus was indeed true. In fact, Luke wants everyone who reads his writings to develop a deeper trust in Jesus as the Messiah, and to see how God fulfilled his plan for humanity through him. In Acts, Luke desires his readers to see the continuing work of Jesus Christ through his disciples as the Holy Spirit guides them. Acts challenges us to believe in Jesus as Messiah, resulting in an active faith that compels us to be a part of his continuing work in our world.

## THE HOLY SPIRIT IN THE
## CONTINUING WORK OF THE CHURCH

Both Luke and Acts emphasize the work of the Holy Spirit. Some suggest a better title for what we know as the Acts of the Apostles would be "the Acts of the Holy Spirit." Luke shows how the Holy Spirit guided the early believers to facilitate the expansion of God's kingdom. The Holy Spirit fills the believers in the upper room on Pentecost. The Holy Spirit fills Peter as he speaks before the Sanhedrin. The Holy Spirit guides Philip to the Ethiopian court official. The Holy Spirit comes upon the Gentiles, leading Peter and his companions to baptize them into Christ. Luke wants his readers to know that Jesus is active in his church through the guidance of the Holy Spirit. More than forty times in Acts, Luke identifies the Holy Spirit as the one who guides the action. Acts challenges us to seek the guidance of God's Holy Spirit as we continue to live out God's redemptive story.

## BREAKING DOWN BARRIERS

Acts tells of the kingdom of God breaking down barrier after barrier. First, the apostles teach the message of salvation to Jews of many nations, breaking the barrier of language at Pentecost. Philip preaches the good news of Jesus to the Samaritans, breaking a social barrier hundreds of years in the making. The Ethiopian eunuch's conversion breaks several barriers. Then Cornelius and his household become participants in God's kingdom—God generously gives the Holy Spirit to Gentiles! Then through the efforts of Paul and others, the gospel spreads throughout the known world. Acts challenges us to be barrier-breakers with our faith—to reach out to all of every nation with the good news of life in Christ Jesus, starting with the neighbor across the street and the homeless on the street corner.

## AN INVITATION TO PARTICIPATE
## IN GOD'S REDEMPTIVE STORY

Luke-Acts is an invitation for readers to participate in God's true intent for our lives. Jesus came to initiate God's rule on this earth, to demonstrate the nature of life in the kingdom of God. He died and was raised according to the will of God in order to establish God's kingdom in this world through his disciples, now guided by the Holy

Spirit. We see how those early believers responded to the gospel. They embodied Jesus. They became Jesus to their world. Peter and John stood boldly before the Sanhedrin, as did Jesus. Stephen willingly laid down his life with language hauntingly familiar to those who know the story of Jesus' death. Peter called Dorcas to life with almost the exact same words Jesus spoke when he raised Jairus' daughter from her death. Luke intentionally uses language that connects the work of those of "the Way" directly to Jesus.

First, Peter embodies Jesus as he reaches out to new peoples with the good news of the kingdom. Then Paul continues Jesus' work, spreading the gospel throughout Asia Minor into Europe. As Acts concludes, Paul is preaching the gospel in Rome while under house arrest. Why end the story here? Was this simply the moment in history in which Luke wrote the story? Could he not have added information about the eventual death of Paul?

This is perhaps where we find Luke's primary purpose for writing. He chooses to end the story not with a period but with a dot, dot, dot. As God broke into history through the life, death, resurrection and ascension of his only Son, providing a way of redemption for all, he continued his work in the world through those amazing first followers of "the Way." Even though the Romans eventually executed Paul, this was not part of Luke's story—because his narrative is not about Paul. Rather, it is the compelling story of the gospel spreading to the ends of the earth as Jesus had promised in Acts 1:8. The story does not end in Rome. It continues through the life of every believer who understands his or her ultimate purpose in God's kingdom.

This is the challenge of Acts. Luke invites each of us to become God's instrument for expanding the borders of his kingdom. Thus we open Acts not just to read what once was, but to direct our thinking about what we should be and do. Will we stand with the courage given by the Spirit and proclaim the good news of Jesus to all? Can we say with Paul, as he stood before King Agrippa and many of the dignitaries of Caesarea, "I pray God that not only you but all who are listening to me today may become what I am"? Paul was so elated with his role in the expansion of the kingdom he could not even think of defending himself—all he could do was proclaim how wonderful it was to be a participant in God's eternal kingdom. Our God invites us into this incredible adventure. Read these texts as if it is your life story—because it is. Let that journey begin!

"Lord, open our eyes and hearts to the thrilling story of the beginning of your church, so that we might continue the story of the expansion of your kingdom through our life."

# THE END OF THE BEGINNING
## (ACTS 1)

## DAY ONE READING AND QUESTIONS

[1] In my former book, Theophilus, I wrote about all that Jesus began to do and to teach [2] until the day he was taken up to heaven, after giving instructions through the Holy Spirit to the apostles he had chosen. [3] After his suffering, he showed himself to these men and gave many convincing proofs that he was alive. He appeared to them over a period of forty days and spoke about the kingdom of God.

*1. What was the content of Luke's gospel as he describes it to Theophilus?*

*2. After his resurrection, Jesus appeared for a period of forty days. Of what did he speak?*

*3. Is the kingdom of God the main thing we have on our minds? If not, why not?*

## DAY TWO READING AND QUESTIONS

[4] On one occasion, while he was eating with them, he gave them this command: "Do not leave Jerusalem, but wait for the gift my Father promised, which you have heard me speak about. [5] For John

baptized with water, but in a few days you will be baptized with the Holy Spirit." [6] So when they met together, they asked him, "Lord, are you at this time going to restore the kingdom to Israel?" [7] He said to them: "It is not for you to know the times or dates the Father has set by his own authority. [8] But you will receive power when the Holy Spirit comes on you; and you will be my witnesses in Jerusalem, and in all Judea and Samaria, and to the ends of the earth."

*1. What gift did the Father promise?*

*2. What do you think the disciples were expecting when they asked if God was about to restore the kingdom of Israel?*

*3. What application does this command "to wait" have in our present day relationship with Jesus?*

## DAY THREE READING AND QUESTIONS

[9] After he said this, he was taken up before their very eyes, and a cloud hid him from their sight. [10] They were looking intently up into the sky as he was going, when suddenly two men dressed in white stood beside them. [11] "Men of Galilee," they said, "why do you stand here looking into the sky? This same Jesus, who has been taken from you into heaven, will come back in the same way you have seen him go into heaven." [12] Then they returned to Jerusalem from the hill called the Mt. of Olives, a Sabbath day's walk from the city. [13] When they arrived, they went upstairs to the room where they were staying. Those present were Peter, John, James and Andrew; Philip and Thomas, Bartholomew and Matthew; James son of Alphaeus and Simon the Zealot, and Judas son of James. [14] They all joined together constantly in prayer, along with the women and Mary the mother of Jesus, and with his brothers.

*1. What do you think the disciples were thinking as Jesus ascended?*

*2. What was the message of the angels?*

*3. Do you live in joyful anticipation of the Lord's return? Why or why not?*

## DAY FOUR READING AND QUESTIONS

[15] In those days Peter stood up among the believers (a group number-ing about a hundred and twenty) [16] and said, "Brothers, the Scripture had to be fulfilled which the Holy Spirit spoke long ago through the mouth of David concerning Judas, who served as guide for those who arrested Jesus— [17] he was one of our number and shared in this ministry." [18] (With the reward he got for his wickedness, Judas bought a field; there he fell headlong, his body burst open and all his intestines spilled out. [19] Everyone in Jerusalem heard about this, so they called that field in their language Akeldama, that is, Field of Blood.) [20] "For," said Peter, "it is written in the book of Psalms, "'May his place be deserted; let there be no one to dwell in it,' and, "'May another take his place of leadership.' [21] Therefore it is necessary to choose one of the men who have been with us the whole time the Lord Jesus went in and out among us, [22] beginning from John's baptism to the time when Jesus was taken up from us. For one of these must become a witness with us of his resurrection." [23] So they proposed two men: Joseph called Barsabbas (also known as Justus) and Matthias. [24] Then they prayed, "Lord, you know everyone's heart. Show us which of these two you have chosen [25] to take over this apostolic ministry, which Judas left to go where he belongs." [26] Then they cast lots, and the lot fell to Matthias; so he was added to the eleven apostles.

*1. What were the requirements for the one who would replace Judas? Why do you think these were necessary?*

*2. How did the disciples choose between Barsabbas and Matthias? How is this a demonstration of faith?*

*3. What does this event (replacing Judas) tell us about what the apostles thought of God's active participation in their lives?*

## DAY FIVE READING AND QUESTIONS

Reread the entire passage (Acts 1:1-26)

*1. What is "the great commission" as Acts records it?*

*2. Why do you think the apostles still wanted Israel to be restored?*

*3. How does considering this story as your story change the way you will read the text?*

# MEDITATION

What an amazing and wonderful story! Jesus has risen from the grave and given many convincing proofs that he is alive. He instructed his followers to stay in Jerusalem until they were baptized with the Holy Spirit. Even after the resurrection, the apostles did not understand the true nature of the kingdom. They still wanted to know if Israel was about to be restored in its former power. Their dreams were too small. God's plan for his kingdom was so much more than they expected. They were its first ambassadors—witnesses of Jesus not only in

Jerusalem and Judea, but to the ends of the earth. A kingdom, indeed!

What was it like to hear Jesus' final words and watch him ascend into the clouds? The voice of an angel asked the apostles to quit standing and looking and to get busy with the Lord's instructions. Luke intends for us to ask, "Have we heard the Lord's instructions to us? Are we full of his Spirit and acting as his witnesses to the world?" The story of Jesus' ascension and the pouring out of the Spirit are not limited to that moment in history. Jesus is risen, his Spirit is in us, and we are to be about his work.

What did the disciples do as they waited for the outpouring of the Spirit? They were all in constant prayer. Can you imagine the sense of anticipation they must have felt? For what do you think they were praying? It would bless today's church to spend time together in fervent anticipatory prayer. Watch for pictures of the early church as we read through Acts. Look specifically for the things the early believers did when they came together. They will pray together, eat together, praise God together, weep together, and celebrate together. What can we learn from this?

We continue to see, as in Luke's gospel, that God does amazing things through common and imperfect people. The Perfect One has left, and yet he has not left us alone. Rather than the end of Christ's work on this earth, this is merely the beginning of a story that is transforming the world. A room full of ordinary people who have experienced the life and teachings of Jesus are about to receive extraordinary power. Ordinary people, transformed into faithful witnesses of God through the power of the Holy Spirit—this is our story.

"Oh, Lord, bless me with a vision of what is truly important. As I enjoy each day of life you give me, may I prayfully be about your work, joyfully anticipating Jesus' return."

# SPIRIT EMPOWERMENT AND NEW COMMUNITY

## (ACTS 2)

## DAY ONE READING AND QUESTIONS

[1] When the day of Pentecost came, they were all together in one place. [2] Suddenly a sound like the blowing of a violent wind came from heaven and filled the whole house where they were sitting. [3] They saw what seemed to be tongues of fire that separated and came to rest on each of them. [4] All of them were filled with the Holy Spirit and began to speak in other tongues as the Spirit enabled them. [5] Now there were staying in Jerusalem God-fearing Jews from every nation under heaven. [6] When they heard this sound, a crowd came together in bewilderment, because each one heard them speaking in his own language. [7] Utterly amazed, they asked: "Are not all these men who are speaking Galileans? [8] Then how is it that each of us hears them in his own native language? [9] Parthians, Medes and Elamites; residents of Mesopotamia, Judea and Cappadocia, Pontus and Asia, [10] Phrygia and Pamphylia, Egypt and the parts of Libya near Cyrene; visitors from Rome [11] (both Jews and converts to Judaism); Cretans and Arabs—we hear them declaring the wonders of God in our own tongues!" [12] Amazed and perplexed, they asked one another, "What does this mean?" [13] Some, however, made fun of them and said, "They have had too much wine."

*1. Why is it significant that the Holy Spirit came on Pentecost?*

*2. What was the message of those filled with the Holy Spirit?*

*3. If you had the ability to speak to a people in their language, what would you first discuss with them? Why?*

## DAY TWO READING AND QUESTIONS

[14] Then Peter stood up with the Eleven, raised his voice and addressed the crowd: "Fellow Jews and all of you who live in Jerusalem, let me explain this to you; listen carefully to what I say. [15] These men are not drunk, as you suppose. It's only nine in the morning! [16] No, this is what was spoken by the prophet Joel: [17] "'In the last days, God says, I will pour out my Spirit on all people. Your sons and daughters will prophesy, your young men will see visions, your old men will dream dreams. [18] Even on my servants, both men and women, I will pour out my Spirit in those days, and they will prophesy. [19] I will show wonders in the heaven above and signs on the earth below, blood and fire and billows of smoke. [20] The sun will be turned to darkness and the moon to blood before the coming of the great and glorious day of the Lord. [21] And everyone who calls on the name of the Lord will be saved.' [22]"Men of Israel, listen to this: Jesus of Nazareth was a man accredited by God to you by miracles, wonders and signs, which God did among you through him, as you yourselves know. [23] This man was handed over to you by God's set purpose and foreknowledge; and you, with the help of wicked men, put him to death by nailing him to the cross. [24] But God raised him from the dead, freeing him from the agony of death, because it was impossible for death to keep its hold on him. [25]David said about him: "'I saw the Lord always before me. Because he is at my right hand, I will not be shaken. [26] Therefore my

heart is glad and my tongue rejoices; my body also will live in hope, [27] because you will not abandon me to the grave, nor will you let your Holy One see decay. [28] You have made known to me the paths of life; you will fill me with joy in your presence.' [29] "Brothers, I can tell you confidently that the patriarch David died and was buried, and his tomb is here to this day. [30] But he was a prophet and knew that God had promised him on oath that he would place one of his descendants on his throne. [31] Seeing what was ahead, he spoke of the resurrection of the Christ, that he was not abandoned to the grave, nor did his body see decay. [32] God has raised this Jesus to life, and we are all witnesses of the fact. [33] Exalted to the right hand of God, he has received from the Father the promised Holy Spirit and has poured out what you now see and hear. [34] For David did not ascend to heaven, and yet he said, "'The Lord said to my Lord: "Sit at my right hand [35] until I make your enemies a footstool for your feet." [36] "Therefore let all Israel be assured of this: God has made this Jesus, whom you crucified, both Lord and Christ."

1. *Imagine you were one who just weeks before had shouted, "Crucify him!" How do you think you would have reacted to Peter's sermon?*

2. *What does it mean to acknowledge Jesus as both "Lord" and "Christ?"*

3. *What visible signs in your life indicate you acknowledge Jesus as Lord and Christ?*

## DAY THREE READING AND QUESTIONS

[37] When the people heard this, they were cut to the heart and said to Peter and the other apostles, "Brothers, what shall we do?" [38] Peter

replied, "Repent and be baptized, every one of you, in the name of Jesus Christ for the forgiveness of your sins. And you will receive the gift of the Holy Spirit. [39] The promise is for you and your children and for all who are far off—for all whom the Lord our God will call." [40] With many other words he warned them; and he pleaded with them, "Save yourselves from this corrupt generation." [41] Those who accepted his message were baptized, and about three thousand were added to their number that day.

1. *Are you surprised at the response of the crowd?*

2. *Try shouting aloud the question asked by the crowd. Use the intonation you think they would have used. How do you think they felt as they asked the question?*

3. *Have you ever felt deeply convicted by your sin to the point that you cried out to God for his mercy and forgiveness?*

## DAY FOUR READING AND QUESTIONS

[42] They devoted themselves to the apostles' teaching and to the fellowship, to the breaking of bread and to prayer. [43] Everyone was filled with awe, and many wonders and miraculous signs were done by the apostles. [44] All the believers were together and had everything in common. [45] Selling their possessions and goods, they gave to anyone as he had need. [46] Every day they continued to meet together in the temple courts. They broke bread in their homes and ate together with glad and sincere hearts, [47] praising God and enjoying the favor of all the people. And the Lord added to their number daily those who were being saved.

1. *What do you think caused the believers' "new-found" devotion? To what were they devoted?*

2. *Why do you think these early believers sought to be together at every available moment? Can we recover this kind of dynamic fellowship today? How?*

3. *Why was that early community of faith attractive to the people around them? Does this say anything to us about how to be effective in sharing the gospel in our culture?*

## DAY FIVE READING

Reread the entire passage (Acts 2:1-47)

1. *What would it have been like to witness these events and hear this teaching?*

2. *Of what specific thing do you think Peter would call us to repent today?*

3. *Do you think it is possible to have a community of faith in today's world that would be as selfless and generous as that first community? Why or why not? What would we, as a church, have to do to have such a way of life?*

## MEDITATION

The Holy Spirit descended on Jesus at his baptism and guided him throughout his earthly ministry. Now, the Spirit descends from heaven onto Jesus' disciples to lead them to continue the Lord's ministry. For Luke, it is the Holy Spirit who assures that God's work through Jesus will continue in his church. Jesus is alive in his church through the Holy Spirit. The perfect Lamb of God was slain during Passover in fulfillment of God's plan for redemption, and now the Holy Spirit is given on Pentecost as a continuing part of the plan. On a day when the Jews celebrated God's full provision for all of their needs, God gave an even greater gift—his Spirit.

The Spirit's arrival caused quite a stir! Hearing the noise of a violent wind, a large multi-national group (still in Jerusalem from the Passover feast and awaiting Pentecost) quickly gathered. Amazingly, simple, uneducated Galileans (known for their lack of education and their inability to speak other languages well) were flawlessly speaking in many different languages. What was all this about?

Peter explained. He began by telling them that the miraculous signs they were witnessing were those promised at the beginning of the Messianic Age. That most anticipated moment had arrived—Messiah had come. However, instead of rejoicing, the message ripped their hearts open—they understood that they had crucified him. They were desperate when they fell to their knees and pleaded, "What shall we do?"

As expected, they would have to die. However, God was not calling for their death as punishment but as a way to new life in his kingdom. Because God had a purpose for their redeemed lives, he forgave them. As Jesus died and was raised, they too were invited to die (through baptism) and be raised to new life—a life of salvation from the meaningless and directionless lives they had lived.

Those accepting the good news formed a marvelous new community. Now living among his people through the Holy Spirit, God removed the enmity that naturally separated them from each other. The change was dramatic and immediate. Believers devoted themselves to the apostles' teaching and to true community (fellowship). They ate together, prayed together, and gave what they had to one another. Eden was "replanted" that day. God moved among his people who were no longer divided by language or social status. There remained many other barriers yet to be broken, but true community had begun. The gracious hand of God overcame the pride and confusion of Babel.

The battles are not over. There will be heartbreaks even in the story of the early church as told by Luke. But this is the picture of the new community of faith for which Jesus Christ died. Can we, like them, realize how desperately we need the grace of God? Are we any different from those who first heard this message of hope? Would we be guilty of crucifying Jesus by the self-focused and materialistic lives we live? What do you think Peter would preach to us today if he came to our churches or into our homes? We need to hear his words anew, "Therefore, let all be assured of this: God has made this Jesus whom you crucified both Lord and Christ."

What shall we do? Repent—the good news is still available. Hear Peter's words as his teaching continues, "Save yourselves from this corrupt generation."

"Precious Lord, open my heart to that from which I must repent in order to fully experience the new life to which you have called me."

# "WHAT WE HAVE WE WILL GIVE"
## (ACTS 3)

## DAY ONE READING AND QUESTIONS

[1] One day Peter and John were going up to the temple at the time of prayer—at three in the afternoon. [2] Now a man crippled from birth

was being carried to the temple gate called Beautiful, where he was put every day to beg from those going into the temple courts. [3] When he saw Peter and John about to enter, he asked them for money. [4]Peter looked straight at him, as did John. Then Peter said, "Look at us!" [5] So the man gave them his attention, expecting to get something from them. [6] Then Peter said, "Silver or gold I do not have, but what I have I give you. In the name of Jesus Christ of Nazareth, walk." [7] Taking him by the right hand, he helped him up, and instantly the man's feet and ankles became strong. [8] He jumped to his feet and began to walk. Then he went with them into the temple courts, walking and jumping, and praising God.

> 1. *Why were Peter and John going to the temple? What does this tell us about their daily practices?*

> 2. *Why do you think Peter told the man to look at them?*

> 3. *Do you notice the beggar along the road? What is your response? Why?*

## DAY TWO READING AND QUESTIONS

[9] When all the people saw him walking and praising God, [10] they recognized him as the same man who used to sit begging at the temple gate called Beautiful, and they were filled with wonder and amazement at what had happened to him. [11] While the beggar held on to Peter and John, all the people were astonished and came running to them in the place called Solomon's Colonnade. [12] When Peter saw this, he said to them: "Men of Israel, why does this surprise you? Why do you stare at us as if by our own power or godliness we had made this man walk? [13] The God of Abraham, Isaac and Jacob, the God of our

fathers, has glorified his servant Jesus. You handed him over to be killed, and you disowned him before Pilate, though he had decided to let him go. [14] You disowned the Holy and Righteous One and asked that a murderer be released to you. [15] You killed the author of life, but God raised him from the dead. We are witnesses of this. [16] By faith in the name of Jesus, this man whom you see and know was made strong. It is Jesus' name and the faith that comes through him that has given this complete healing to him, as you can all see.

*1. What was the people's reaction to the beggar's healing?*

*2. Why do you think the beggar "held" on to Peter and John?*

*3. Read Peter's words out loud. What effect does this simple message have on you? How would you have responded had you been there?*

## DAY THREE READING AND QUESTIONS

[17] "Now, brothers, I know that you acted in ignorance, as did your leaders. [18] But this is how God fulfilled what he had foretold through all the prophets, saying that his Christ would suffer. [19] Repent, then, and turn to God, so that your sins may be wiped out, that times of refreshing may come from the Lord, [20] and that he may send the Christ, who has been appointed for you— even Jesus. [21] He must remain in heaven until the time comes for God to restore everything, as he promised long ago through his holy prophets. [22] For Moses said, 'The Lord your God will raise up for you a prophet like me from among your own people; you must listen to everything he tells you. [23] Anyone who does not listen to him will be completely cut off from among his people.'

*1. Is it significant that Peter called his listeners "brothers"? Why or why not?*

*2. Why was the idea of the Christ suffering so foreign to them? Why were they not able to see this in the writings of the prophets?*

*3. Why are Moses' words important in this passage?*

## DAY FOUR READING AND QUESTIONS

[24] "Indeed, all the prophets from Samuel on, as many as have spoken, have foretold these days. [25] And you are heirs of the prophets and of the covenant God made with your fathers. He said to Abraham, 'Through your offspring all peoples on earth will be blessed.' [26] When God raised up his servant, he sent him first to you to bless you by turning each of you from your wicked ways.

*1. Of what did all the prophets speak? Why hadn't they been heard?*

*2. How would God's servant bless the Jews to whom Peter was speaking? What did they have to do in order to receive the blessing?*

*3. Do you see yourself as an heir to the promises of God? What do we have to do in order to receive these blessings?*

## DAY FIVE READING AND QUESTIONS

Reread the entire passage (Acts 3:1-26)

*1. If you were going to write a continuation of this story, what do you think the healed man did in the succeeding days?*

*2. Are there things in your life that cripple your faith? Have you asked God for healing through the powerful name of Jesus?*

*3. Do you walk, run, and leap as you praise God for the healing you have received in Jesus Christ? Do we experience the "times of refreshing" from the Lord? Why or why not?*

# MEDITATION

New life in Jesus Christ—it was good news then, it is good news now. What does Luke want us to experience through the healing miracles of Jesus and his followers? Did Luke not tell us that Jesus was the fulfillment of God's promise, that he would give sight to the blind and allow the lame to walk (Luke 4:18, 19)? We should not be surprised that in Acts this healing ministry continues through the followers of Jesus. These miracles are always much more than physical healings. They are by nature restorative—they bring people back into a life of meaning and purpose, allowing them to participate fully in God's creational intent for their lives.

Peter and John continue the healing work of Jesus. Perhaps initially disappointed not to receive money, the crippled beggar instead receives something of infinitely greater value—full restoration to life. This is an unbelievable miracle! Never having walked—never— he was not only made strong enough to walk, but even to jump. And jump he did, praising God for his new life. All who observed this were amazed. Visualize this man, looking with amazement at his "new legs" jumping and shouting and praising God. What joy there must have been in the temple courts that day!

Peter's response is surprising. Reacting to the people's amazement he said, in effect, "So what?" He continued, "Do you think we did this? No, the God who raised Jesus the Christ from the grave is the one who has healed this man completely. Now look, we know you were not aware of what you were doing when you killed Jesus. All you need to do is repent of your former life, and turn to God, and he will wipe your sins away. You, too, can experience such times of refreshing."

Acts continually calls us to place ourselves in the story. Are we the apostles who have seen Jesus and know the truth? Are we the crippled man at the gate? Are we the people amazed at his healing? Either we are the proclaimers of the great news of the kingdom or those challenged to turn from their wicked ways. The one who allowed the crippled man to jump for joy with a heart of praise can bring new life to us, wherever we might be. What good news! Times of refreshing in the Lord await those who will repent.

"Lord, thank you for the wonderful news of your kingdom! I acknowledge the healing of my spirit by the blood of Jesus with great and visible joy."

# A COURAGEOUS STAND
## (ACTS 4:1-31)

### DAY ONE READING AND QUESTIONS

[1] The priests and the captain of the temple guard and the Sadducees came up to Peter and John while they were speaking to the people. [2] They were greatly disturbed because the apostles were teaching the people and proclaiming in Jesus the resurrection of the dead. [3] They seized Peter and John, and because it was evening, they

put them in jail until the next day. <sup>4</sup> But many who heard the message believed, and the number of men grew to about five thousand.

<sup>5</sup> The next day the rulers, elders and teachers of the law met in Jerusalem. <sup>6</sup> Annas the high priest was there, and so were Caiaphas, John, Alexander and the other men of the high priest's family. <sup>7</sup> They had Peter and John brought before them and began to question them: "By what power or what name did you do this?"

*1. What teaching greatly disturbed the Sadducees? Why?*

*2. What question did the rulers ask Peter and John? Does this remind you of questions asked of Jesus?*

*3. Is there any activity so clearly founded in the name and heart of Jesus in our lives that some might ask us to explain ourselves? If so, what?*

## DAY TWO READING AND QUESTIONS

<sup>8</sup> Then Peter, filled with the Holy Spirit, said to them: "Rulers and elders of the people! <sup>9</sup> If we are being called to account today for an act of kindness shown to a cripple and are asked how he was healed, <sup>1</sup>then know this, you and all the people of Israel: It is by the name of Jesus Christ of Nazareth, whom you crucified but whom God raised from the dead, that this man stands before you healed. <sup>11</sup> He is "'the stone you builders rejected, which has become the capstone.' <sup>12</sup> Salvation is found in no one else, for there is no other name under heaven given to men by which we must be saved." <sup>13</sup> When they saw the courage of Peter and John and realized that they were unschooled, ordinary men, they were astonished and they took note that these men had been with Jesus. <sup>14</sup> But since they could see the man who had been healed standing there with them, there was nothing they could say.

1. *How did Peter's "filling with the Holy Spirit" affect him? Does this remind you of any promises Jesus specifically made to his disciples about the work of the Holy Spirit in them?*

2. *Why is "the name of Jesus" such an important topic? Do we live "in the name of Jesus?*

3. *What fact astonished the assembly? When the world looks at us, is there any aspect of our lives that would astonish?*

## DAY THREE READING AND QUESTIONS

[15] So they ordered them to withdraw from the Sanhedrin and then conferred together. [16] "What are we going to do with these men?" they asked. "Everybody living in Jerusalem knows they have done an outstanding miracle, and we cannot deny it. [17] But to stop this thing from spreading any further among the people, we must warn these men to speak no longer to anyone in this name." [18] Then they called them in again and commanded them not to speak or teach at all in the name of Jesus. [19] But Peter and John replied, "Judge for yourselves whether it is right in God's sight to obey you rather than God. [20] For we cannot help speaking about what we have seen and heard." [21] After further threats they let them go. They could not decide how to punish them, because all the people were praising God for what had happened. [22] For the man who was miraculously healed was over forty years old.

1. *Why would those of the Sanhedrin want to deny the miracle of healing the cripple?*

2. *What was their concern about "the name" of Jesus of Nazareth?*

*3. Is our experience of salvation in Jesus such that we "cannot help" from talking about it to all we see and know? If not, why not? How can such fire be kindled in our hearts?*

## DAY FOUR READING AND QUESTIONS

²³ On their release, Peter and John went back to their own people and reported all that the chief priests and elders had said to them. ²⁴When they heard this, they raised their voices together in prayer to God. "Sovereign Lord," they said, "you made the heaven and the earth and the sea, and everything in them. ²⁵ You spoke by the Holy Spirit through the mouth of your servant, our father David: "'Why do the nations rage and the peoples plot in vain? ²⁶ The kings of the earth take their stand and the rulers gather together against the Lord and against his Anointed One.' ²⁷ Indeed Herod and Pontius Pilate met together with the Gentiles and the people of Israel in this city to conspire against your holy servant Jesus, whom you anointed. ²⁸ They did what your power and will had decided beforehand should happen. ²⁹ Now, Lord, consider their threats and enable your servants to speak your word with great boldness. ³⁰ Stretch out your hand to heal and perform miraculous signs and wonders through the name of your holy servant Jesus." ³¹ After they prayed, the place where they were meeting was shaken. And they were all filled with the Holy Spirit and spoke the word of God boldly.

*1. Does the reaction of the church surprise you? Do you think we would react in a similar way if one of our own was imprisoned and threatened?*

*2. What did they acknowledge together about the powers of wickedness and the plan of God?*

*3. Do we see God at work even in the evil of our time? What can we do to recover the confidence that God is at work in all events?*

## DAY FIVE READING AND QUESTIONS

Reread the entire passage (Acts 4:1-31)

*1. How much courage do you have in sharing your faith? Explain.*

*2. Do we see ourselves as participants in God's redemptive story— today? Why or why not?*

*3. What can we do as a church and as individuals to learn to suffer with joy rather than complaining about every small inconvenience?*

## MEDITATION

It was just a matter of time. Three thousand first obeyed the good news of Jesus Christ. Now, an amazing miracle has occurred, and even more have come to belief—the number of men who believed was now over five thousand. With all this commotion around the temple, the "spiritual police" had to show up. The Sadducees, who were the wealthiest and most influential sect of the Jews, led the group. They also did not believe in the resurrection, which was at the core of what Peter and John were preaching. They could not permit this to continue—so they had Peter and John thrown into jail for the night.

The next day, they brought Peter and John before them and asked, "By what power or name did you do this?" Of course, they were referring to the healing of the crippled man. This gives Luke the opportunity to tell us the story again. Yes, Peter is speaking, but Luke is writing. He has already allowed Peter to tell us the story of Jesus twice, but we will hear it repeatedly throughout Acts. He wants us to hear the story over and over until we embrace it fully and experience the joy of life in the kingdom. Here is the story—healing is in the precious name of Jesus Christ. Salvation is found in no one else.

Peter's words are unsettling in our world of religious pluralism. How can we say that salvation is found only in Jesus Christ? Peter could say it because he and John embodied it. They were living it. They knew it was true. Even those completely opposed to them had to be impressed with these unschooled, ordinary men forever changed because they had been with Jesus. Peter, who cowered in fear before the accusations of a slave girl just weeks before, now stood boldly and proclaimed new life in Jesus. Even after having been threatened, both he and John said, "We cannot help but speak about what we have seen and heard."

Salvation is not something someone receives at death. It is life in the kingdom of God available only through Christ Jesus. Salvation is life that radically changes us, because the Holy Spirit controls our lives and transforms us into the image of Jesus. What keeps us from proclaiming such truths? What or whom do we fear? As the crippled man jumped with joy and praise, so Peter and John celebrated their healed lives with acclamations of praise no power on earth could silence.

The response of the believing community is revealing. After being threatened, Peter and John went back to "their own people." Their response was not fear, only praise. Prayers for boldness replaced the natural response of fear. In this praise and prayer was a crucial acknowledgement—God was sovereign indeed! Let the nations rage, let the kings take their stand—who will stop the Lord's anointed ones?

What has changed for us in our time and place in history? Is God not sovereign? Why do we fear? Where is our bold proclamation that Jesus is Lord?

"Sovereign Lord, fill us with courage and the conviction to profess boldly and lovingly the good news of Jesus."

41

# SELFLESS AND SELF-GLORIFYING GIVING
## (ACTS 4:32-5:16)

### DAY ONE READING AND QUESTIONS

[32] All the believers were one in heart and mind. No one claimed that any of his possessions was his own, but they shared everything they had. [33] With great power the apostles continued to testify to the resurrection of the Lord Jesus, and much grace was upon them all. [34] There were no needy persons among them. For from time to time those who owned lands or houses sold them, brought the money from the sales [35] and put it at the apostles' feet, and it was distributed to anyone as he had need. [36] Joseph, a Levite from Cyprus, whom the apostles called Barnabas (which means Son of Encouragement), [37] sold a field he owned and brought the money and put it at the apostles' feet.

1. *Why is it significant that there were no needy people among the believers?*

2. *Why do you think the believers gave their money to the apostles when lands or houses were sold?*

3. *Do you think the church should return to this kind of generous giving? If so, how? If not, why not?*

## DAY TWO READING AND QUESTIONS

[1] Now a man named Ananias, together with his wife Sapphira, also sold a piece of property. [2] With his wife's full knowledge he kept back part of the money for himself, but brought the rest and put it at the apostles' feet. [3] Then Peter said, "Ananias, how is it that Satan has so filled your heart that you have lied to the Holy Spirit and have kept for yourself some of the money you received for the land? [4] Didn't it belong to you before it was sold? And after it was sold, wasn't the money at your disposal? What made you think of doing such a thing? You have not lied to men but to God." [5] When Ananias heard this, he fell down and died. And great fear seized all who heard what had happened. [6] Then the young men came forward, wrapped up his body, and carried him out and buried him.

*1. What do you think was going on in Ananias' and Sapphira's hearts to spur them to do what they did?*

*2. Why was their behavior such a serious offense?*

*3. In what sense did Ananias lie to God? Can we lie to God in similar ways?*

## DAY THREE READING AND QUESTIONS

[7] About three hours later his wife came in, not knowing what had happened. [8] Peter asked her, "Tell me, is this the price you and Ananias got for the land?" "Yes," she said, "that is the price." [9] Peter said to her, "How could you agree to test the Spirit of the Lord? Look! The feet of the men who buried your husband are at the door, and

they will carry you out also." [10] At that moment she fell down at his feet and died. Then the young men came in and, finding her dead, carried her out and buried her beside her husband. [11] Great fear seized the whole church and all who heard about these events.

*1. Why do you think Luke tells of Ananias and Sapphira separately?*

*2. In what way did Sapphira agree to "test the Spirit of the Lord"?*

*3. What can we learn from this episode in the life of the early church?*

## DAY FOUR READING AND QUESTIONS

[12] The apostles performed many miraculous signs and wonders among the people. And all the believers used to meet together in Solomon's Colonnade. [13] No one else dared join them, even though they were highly regarded by the people. [14] Nevertheless, more and more men and women believed in the Lord and were added to their number. [15]As a result, people brought the sick into the streets and laid them on beds and mats so that at least Peter's shadow might fall on some of them as he passed by. [16] Crowds gathered also from the towns around Jerusalem, bringing their sick and those tormented by evil spirits, and all of them were healed.

*1. Did the deaths of Ananias and Sapphira affect the growth of the church? How?*

*2. Why did people highly regard the believers? What do we need to do to receive that same regard today?*

*3. What influence do you think God intends for His church to have in today's world? Does the church have that kind of influence? Why or why not?*

## DAY FIVE READING AND QUESTIONS

Reread the entire passage (Acts 4:32-5:11)

1. *Do you know a modern-day "Barnabas"? Describe this person and identify what allows them to be generous and encouraging.*

2. *Have you been guilty of "hidden-motive" giving? If so, how did it make you feel? What can you do to avoid falling to this temptation in the future?*

3. *How can we learn to be God-focused instead of self-focused in the good that we do?*

## MEDITATION

What a thrill it must have been to be a part of this community! Jesus was indeed alive in his church. People were continuing to sell their possessions and give what they had to meet the needs of this new community. Joseph (whom we better know as Barnabas) was a wonderful example of one who sold a field to give the money to believers in need. One of the powerful teaching techniques in Luke's gospel is comparative stories. It is an effective way of contrasting obedience and disobedience. Luke compares Barnabas to Ananias and Sapphira.

This story is challenging for us because we cannot imagine God striking someone dead for what we might call a "white lie." Ananias and Sapphira, after all, did sell what they once owned in order to do good. However, right action does not mean one's heart is right. Peter identifies their sin—they had lied to the Holy Spirit. In stark contrast to Barnabas—a faithful, God-honoring giver—Ananias and Sapphira were deceitful and desired self-glory. The root of their sin was the love of money and desire for the approval of others.

Whether it was fair for them to be so quickly and decisively judged is not ours to decide. It was the action of God. The more important question is, "Are we sometimes guilty of this same sin?" We need to be honest about our need for others to think well of us, even when not deserved. And what of the sin of greed? Do we have trouble giving generously because we focus on storing up things for ourselves? This need caused the rich young ruler to walk away from Jesus. The impulse for easy money led Judas to betray Jesus and destroy his own life. In the wise words of Jesus, "What worth is it to have the whole world but lose your own life?" In effect, this is what Ananias and Sapphira did. Their temporary material gain led directly to their ultimate loss.

The irony is that honesty would have resolved the crisis. Ananias and Sapphira could have given their gift—and it would have been a generous gift. All they needed to do was to be truthful. "Peter, here is our gift. It is not all we gained from selling the land, but we wanted to give part of what we gained to meet the needs of the church." The problem was not the extent of the gift, but the deceitfulness of the heart. So we ask ourselves the question, "What motivates the good that I do?" Is it to advance the kingdom? If so, honesty must reign. We do not advance the kingdom or help ourselves through deceit. The response to God's judgment on Ananias and Sapphira is interesting. The community of faith had been growing rapidly. With the exception of a little persecution, everything seemed positive. Suddenly we see the importance of living consistently with the purposes of a holy God. Great fear seized not only the church, but all who heard of these events. The effect at first seemed counterproductive, because Luke observes, "no one else dared joined them." But

Luke adds, "Nonetheless, more and more men and women believed in the Lord and were added to their number." How could this be? No one dared join them but they continued to grow. Is this not a contradiction? Not for Luke. His point is that no one casually walked into their midst. It was not an easy step to commit to the kingdom. People who believed understood the radical nature of their repentance; they took the kingdom of God seriously. The result was not only an increase in believers, there was also an increase in ministry opportunities. Large crowds gathered, the sick were healed, and those tormented by evil spirits were freed of their distress. It is as if Jesus were once again walking the streets of Jerusalem. And indeed he was, through his church.

Though not popular to say in these times, we must acknowledge it is a fearful thing to serve our holy God. It is also a joyous life. True joy does not come unless we have a deep, reverential fear of our mighty, yet gracious God. While he is a loving Father, he has a holy purpose for our lives. He has gifted us, blessed us, forgiven us, and equipped us, not for a self-glorifying life of materialism, but for a God-glorifying life of liberal giving and loving service.

Who would we be in this story, Barnabas or Ananias and Sapphira? If the answer is not Barnabas, Peter would challenge us, "Repent, then, and turn to God, so that your sins may be wiped out, that times of refreshing may come from the Lord, and that he may send the Christ, who has been appointed for you—even Jesus" (Acts 3:19-20).

"Loving Lord, fill us with reverent fear for your holy name."

# A COURAGEOUS STAND II
## (ACTS 5:17-42)

## DAY ONE READING AND QUESTIONS

[17] Then the high priest and all his associates, who were members of the party of the Sadducees, were filled with jealousy. [18] They arrested the apostles and put them in the public jail. [19] But during the night an angel of the Lord opened the doors of the jail and brought them out. [20] "Go, stand in the temple courts," he said, "and tell the people the full message of this new life."

*1. Why do you think the leaders were jealous of Peter and the apostles?*

*2. What did the angel tell the apostles to preach? Is this the message we preach?*

*3. Are you excited about the message we have to tell the world? Why or why not?*

## DAY TWO READING AND QUESTIONS

[21] At daybreak they entered the temple courts, as they had been told, and began to teach the people. When the high priest and his associates arrived, they called together the Sanhedrin—the full assembly of

the elders of Israel—and sent to the jail for the apostles. [22] But on arriving at the jail, the officers did not find them there. So they went back and reported, [23] "We found the jail securely locked, with the guards standing at the doors; but when we opened them, we found no one inside." [24] On hearing this report, the captain of the temple guard and the chief priests were puzzled, wondering what would come of this.

1. *Are you surprised at the willingness of Peter and John immediately to preach again?*

2. *What do you make of the response of the leaders to the news of the empty jail cell? What were they thinking?*

3. *Have you ever experienced deliverance that you are sure was from God? If so, recall the experience and your thoughts.*

## DAY THREE READING AND QUESTIONS

[25] Then someone came and said, "Look! The men you put in jail are standing in the temple courts teaching the people." [26] At that, the captain went with his officers and brought the apostles. They did not use force, because they feared that the people would stone them. [27]Having brought the apostles, they made them appear before the Sanhedrin to be questioned by the high priest. [28] "We gave you strict orders not to teach in this name," he said. "Yet you have filled Jerusalem with your teaching and are determined to make us guilty of this man's blood." [29] Peter and the other apostles replied: "We must obey God rather than men! [30] The God of our fathers raised Jesus from the dead—whom you had killed by hanging him on a tree. [31] God exalted him to his own right hand as Prince and Savior that he might give repentance and forgiveness of sins to Israel. [32] We are witnesses of

these things, and so is the Holy Spirit, whom God has given to those who obey him." [33] When they heard this, they were furious and wanted to put them to death.

*1. Why didn't the guards use force to arrest Peter?*

*2. Why do you think Peter's response so infuriated his hearers?*

*3. When is it right to be guilty of civil disobedience?*

## DAY FOUR READING AND QUESTIONS

[34] But a Pharisee named Gamaliel, a teacher of the law, who was honored by all the people, stood up in the Sanhedrin and ordered that the men be put outside for a little while. [35] Then he addressed them: "Men of Israel, consider carefully what you intend to do to these men. [36] Some time ago Theudas appeared, claiming to be somebody, and about four hundred men rallied to him. He was killed, all his followers were dispersed, and it all came to nothing. [37] After him, Judas the Galilean appeared in the days of the census and led a band of people in revolt. He too was killed, and all his followers were scattered. [38] Therefore, in the present case I advise you: Leave these men alone! Let them go! For if their purpose or activity is of human origin, it will fail. [39] But if it is from God, you will not be able to stop these men; you will only find yourselves fighting against God." [40] His speech persuaded them. They called the apostles in and had them flogged. Then they ordered them not to speak in the name of Jesus, and let them go. [41]The apostles left the Sanhedrin, rejoicing because they had been counted worthy of suffering disgrace for the Name. [42] Day after day, in the temple courts and from house to house, they never stopped teaching and proclaiming the good news that Jesus is the Christ.

*1. Why do you think Gamaliel responded as he did?*

*2. Why did the Sanhedrin flog Peter and John even though they accepted Gamaliel's reasoning?*

*3. What was the apostles' response to their flogging? Would this be our response to such persecution? If not, why not?*

## DAY FIVE READING AND QUESTIONS

Reread the entire passage

*1. Have you ever been jealous of one doing good? What was your response? What should it have been?*

*2. What do you think Gamaliel thought about the apostles? Do you think he believed they were of God?*

*3. Are you willing to suffer for "the sake of the Name?" In what ways might we suffer for Jesus in our culture?*

# MEDITATION

Following the troubling episode of Ananias and Sapphira, we return to the main story line of exceptional passion and courage of common folks transformed by God's Spirit. The ministry of the apostles looks similar to the early days of Jesus' work—throngs coming to hear his message, seeking healing for their sick.

Should we be surprised at the jealousy of the religious leaders? Common fishermen were doing things they could not do. They were preaching the dynamic message of God's kingdom. They were performing signs with undeniable power. The people were hanging on their every word and praising God for every miracle. The Sadducees, in particular, would have none of this. They were the leaders in the temple and in society. These Galilean upstarts would not steal their deserved glory. Motivated by petty jealousy, they had them arrested. But no earthly power could stop the work of God. An angel miraculously freed the apostles, saying, "Go and tell the people the full message of this new life."

The next morning the pretentious leaders gathered to pass judgment on these common men. But they confronted a serious problem. The jail was empty. Doors locked, prison undisturbed, just one thing lacking—the prisoners! As we might imagine, this left the chief priests and captain of the guard deeply puzzled. Can you imagine what the leaders must have thought when they received the next report? These men were out there again, right in the middle of things, preaching away. Surely, no one expected this! If somehow these men had bribed their way out of prison, would you not think they would be in southern Syria about now? No, not these men—they knew the power of God had freed them and they were passionate about sharing what they knew to be good news. They had seen the risen Lord. Kill them if you must, but they would not stop speaking of Jesus Christ. So now the captain and his men gingerly moved through the crowd and "suggested" the apostles come with them. They did not use force because of their fear of the crowd's response.

Can you hear the scolding the apostles received from these powerless religious leaders? "We told you not to do this—to preach in this name. What part of 'no' do you not understand?" Even though they were motivated by jealousy, the leaders had now formed a charge against the apostles, "You are trying to make us guilty of 'this man's' blood." They would not use the name of Jesus. And of course, they were guilty of his blood—just as all of us are.

Peter and the apostles responded without hesitation, "We must obey God rather than men." No man or earthly power could repress the good news of kingdom life in Jesus. The answer given by Peter, by the way, was not disrespectful. They acknowledged the power of these leaders, but stated that God himself had trumped it. Their egos now badly battered, this was more than they could stand. Now they wanted the apostles dead (sounds familiar, does it not—this is the way they thought they could rid themselves of Jesus). Gamaliel wisely advised them to leave these men alone. If they were false prophets, they would disappear like the many before them. However, if these men were of God, who could stop them? Surprisingly, this line of reasoning made sense to the leaders. But it did not quell their jealous anger. So they punished the apostles with a flogging and again ordered them to stop speaking about Jesus before releasing them.

So how did the apostles leave the Sanhedrin? Licking their wounds? Cowering before the threats of these mighty leaders? No, they left rejoicing that they had been counted worthy of suffering disgrace for the Name. Picture in your minds the looks on the faces of the religious leaders as they watched Peter and John leave—celebrating! If the apostles could be so brave in the face of threats and beatings, what should we be able to do in our lives free of such threats? Nothing has changed. The Name is still precious. The good news is as valid as ever.

"Oh Lord, once again we pray for the courage to expand your kingdom in the face of every fear we might hold."

# FOCUSED LEADERS AND STEPHEN'S ARREST

## (ACTS 6)

### DAY ONE READING AND QUESTIONS

[1] In those days when the number of disciples was increasing, the Grecian Jews among them complained against the Hebraic Jews because their widows were being overlooked in the daily distribution of food. [2] So the Twelve gathered all the disciples together and said, "It would not be right for us to neglect the ministry of the word of God in order to wait on tables. [3] Brothers, choose seven men from among you who are known to be full of the Spirit and wisdom. We will turn this responsibility over to them [4] and will give our attention to prayer and the ministry of the word."

*1. Why were the apostles unwilling to solve this issue?*

*2. What were to be the characteristics of the men asked to serve in overseeing the distribution of the food?*

*3. What did the apostles see as their primary calling? What can we learn from this for the church of today?*

## DAY TWO READING AND QUESTIONS

⁵ This proposal pleased the whole group. They chose Stephen, a man full of faith and of the Holy Spirit; also Philip, Procorus, Nicanor, Timon, Parmenas, and Nicolas from Antioch, a convert to Judaism. ⁶They presented these men to the apostles, who prayed and laid their hands on them. ⁷ So the word of God spread. The number of disciples in Jerusalem increased rapidly, and a large number of priests became obedient to the faith.

1. *What do you think was the nature of the apostles' prayer for these men?*

2. *What can we learn about how to treat ministry leaders from these verses?*

3. *Why do you think Luke connected the spread of God's word to this action of believers?*

## DAY THREE READING AND QUESTIONS

⁸ Now Stephen, a man full of God's grace and power, did great wonders and miraculous signs among the people. ⁹ Opposition arose, however, from members of the Synagogue of the Freedmen (as it was called)—Jews of Cyrene and Alexandria as well as the provinces of Cilicia and Asia. These men began to argue with Stephen, ¹⁰ but they could not stand up against his wisdom or the Spirit by whom he spoke.

1. *What do you think it looks like when a man is full of God's grace and power?*

*2. What do you think caused the opposition that arose against Stephen?*

*3. How do you respond when others oppose or accuse you? Do you*
*allow the Holy Spirit to guide you in those moments?*

## DAY FOUR READING AND QUESTIONS

[11] Then they secretly persuaded some men to say, "We have heard
Stephen speak words of blasphemy against Moses and against God."
[12] So they stirred up the people and the elders and the teachers of the
law. They seized Stephen and brought him before the Sanhedrin. [13]
They produced false witnesses, who testified, "This fellow never stops
speaking against this holy place and against the law. [14] For we have
heard him say that this Jesus of Nazareth will destroy this place and
change the customs Moses handed down to us." [15] All who were sitting
in the Sanhedrin looked intently at Stephen, and they saw that his
face was like the face of an angel. [7:1] Then the high priest asked him,
"Are these charges true?"

*1. What did Stephen's adversaries do when they could not stand up*
*to his wisdom?*

*2. Has anyone ever falsely accused you? How did you respond?*

*3. Of what does Stephen's treatment remind you?*

## DAY FIVE READING AND QUESTIONS

Reread the entire passage.

*1. Why were the apostles so willing to delegate authority to "the seven"
in order to resolve the Grecian widows' complaint?*

*2. Why did the apostles lay their hands on the seven?*

*3. Why do you think Luke informs us that Stephen's face was like that
of an angel? What do you think he means by this description?*

## MEDITATION

Here another challenge threatens the unity of the community of
faith. The Grecian Jews felt their widows were being overlooked in the
daily distribution of food, while the widows of the Aramaic community were not. When first confronted with the accusation, the apostles
rightly observed that it would be improper for them to be sidetracked
by this issue. It was not that meeting the needs of the Grecian widows
was unimportant. In fact, their response demonstrates just how
important they viewed the issue to be, but it was not proper for them
to resolve it.

The Twelve had a clear sense of their primary responsibilities
within the community. Theirs was a ministry of prayer and of the
word. Accepting other responsibilities would detract them from these.
For this reason they advised the community to select highly qualified
men to determine a plan of action. Each was to be known for being
full of the Spirit and wisdom.

Once chosen, the apostles prayed for them and laid their hands
on them, a sign of blessing and delegation. The result of resolving this
issue in this manner was a continual spreading of the word of God.
Even a large number of priests became obedient to the faith.

As readers, we are full of joy and excitement as we experience
victory after victory, from evils and dangers within and without the

community of faith. But in the next episode, we encounter the martyrdom of Stephen. He was a man full of faith and the Holy Spirit. So much so, in fact, that he quickly made enemies. As he spoke of Jesus, Messiah, a group from a particular synagogue tried to argue with Stephen, but they were no match for one full of God's Spirit.

What did they do? They plotted to have Stephen arrested. Stephen is living the story of Jesus over again. Remember that what Jesus did in Luke's gospel, the apostles and the church do in Acts. In the midst of these false accusations and charges, Stephen remains calm and unmoved, his face like that of an angel. What does that mean? It means he was full of the Holy Spirit. He was full of grace and power. He had the look of one in total control, though he was the one accused. His serenity and confidence unnerved his adversaries. This is not to be confused with a look of smugness or self-righteousness. This is the confident face of Jesus seen in Stephen. Jesus is alive in his church.

Oh, that the world could see his face through us. Are we full of God's grace and power? Then fear and worry has no place in our lives. From the world's point of view, Stephen was in serious trouble. From his own point of view, he was exactly where he should have been.

"Lord, give us wisdom to resolve our disagreements within the body of Christ. May the world see the face of Jesus in all we do and say."

# STEPHEN EMBODIES JESUS
## (ACTS 7)

## DAY ONE READING AND QUESTIONS

[1] Then the high priest asked him, "Are these charges true?" [2] To this he replied: "Brothers and fathers, listen to me! The God of glory appeared to our father Abraham while he was still in Mesopotamia, before he lived in Haran. [3] 'Leave your country and your people,' God said, 'and go to the land I will show you.' [4] "So he left the land of the Chaldeans and settled in Haran. After the death of his father, God sent him to this land where you are now living. [5] He gave him no inheritance here, not even a foot of ground. But God promised him that he and his descendants after him would possess the land, even though at that time Abraham had no child. [6] God spoke to him in this way: 'Your descendants will be strangers in a country not their own, and they will be enslaved and mistreated four hundred years. [7] But I will punish the nation they serve as slaves,' God said, 'and afterward they will come out of that country and worship me in this place.' [8]Then he gave Abraham the covenant of circumcision. And Abraham became the father of Isaac and circumcised him eight days after his birth. Later Isaac became the father of Jacob, and Jacob became the father of the twelve patriarchs. [9] "Because the patriarchs were jealous of Joseph, they sold him as a slave into Egypt. But God was with him [10]and rescued him from all his troubles. He gave Joseph wisdom and enabled him to gain the goodwill of Pharaoh king of Egypt; so he

made him ruler over Egypt and all his palace. [11] "Then a famine struck all Egypt and Canaan, bringing great suffering, and our fathers could not find food. [12] When Jacob heard that there was grain in Egypt, he sent our fathers on their first visit. [13] On their second visit, Joseph told his brothers who he was, and Pharaoh learned about Joseph's family. [14] After this, Joseph sent for his father Jacob and his whole family, seventy-five in all. [15] Then Jacob went down to Egypt, where he and our fathers died. [16] Their bodies were brought back to Shechem and placed in the tomb that Abraham had bought from the sons of Hamor at Shechem for a certain sum of money.

1. *With what greeting does Stephen address his accusers? Why is this significant?*

2. *Though God made great promises to Abraham, what did God tell him about the nature of the blessing (difficult or easy)?*

3. *What does Stephen's telling of God's story inform us about the nature of a God-blessed life?*

## DAY TWO READING AND QUESTIONS

[17] "As the time drew near for God to fulfill his promise to Abraham, the number of our people in Egypt greatly increased. [18] Then another king, who knew nothing about Joseph, became ruler of Egypt. [19] He dealt treacherously with our people and oppressed our forefathers by forcing them to throw out their newborn babies so that they would die. [20] "At that time Moses was born, and he was no ordinary child. For three months he was cared for in his father's house. [21] When he was placed outside, Pharaoh's daughter took him and brought him up as her own son. [22] Moses was educated in all the

wisdom of the Egyptians and was powerful in speech and action. [23] "When Moses was forty years old, he decided to visit his fellow Israelites. [24] He saw one of them being mistreated by an Egyptian, so he went to his defense and avenged him by killing the Egyptian. [25] Moses thought that his own people would realize that God was using him to rescue them, but they did not. [26] The next day Moses came upon two Israelites who were fighting. He tried to reconcile them by saying, 'Men, you are brothers; why do you want to hurt each other?' [27] "But the man who was mistreating the other pushed Moses aside and said, 'Who made you ruler and judge over us? [28] Do you want to kill me as you killed the Egyptian yesterday?' [29] When Moses heard this, he fled to Midian, where he settled as a foreigner and had two sons. [30] "After forty years had passed, an angel appeared to Moses in the flames of a burning bush in the desert near Mount Sinai. [31] When he saw this, he was amazed at the sight. As he went over to look more closely, he heard the Lord's voice: [32] 'I am the God of your fathers, the God of Abraham, Isaac and Jacob.' Moses trembled with fear and did not dare to look. [33] "Then the Lord said to him, 'Take off your sandals; the place where you are standing is holy ground. [34] I have indeed seen the oppression of my people in Egypt. I have heard their groaning and have come down to set them free. Now come, I will send you back to Egypt.' [35] "This is the same Moses whom they had rejected with the words, 'Who made you ruler and judge?' He was sent to be their ruler and deliverer by God himself, through the angel who appeared to him in the bush. [36] He led them out of Egypt and did wonders and miraculous signs in Egypt, at the Red Sea and for forty years in the desert. [37]"This is that Moses who told the Israelites, 'God will send you a prophet like me from your own people.' [38] He was in the assembly in the desert, with the angel who spoke to him on Mount Sinai, and with our fathers; and he received living words to pass on to us.

*1. How does Stephen's retelling of the story of Moses address the accusations made against him? (Acts 6:11)*

*2. How did the Israelites receive Moses when he first tried to help them? How did the Jews of Stephen's day regard Moses?*

*3. Of what promise of God to Moses does Stephen remind his accusers? In what way does Stephen's narration of the Moses story remind you of Jesus?*

## DAY THREE READING AND QUESTIONS

[39] "But our fathers refused to obey him. Instead, they rejected him and in their hearts turned back to Egypt. [40] They told Aaron, 'Make us gods who will go before us. As for this fellow Moses who led us out of Egypt—we don't know what has happened to him!' [41] That was the time they made an idol in the form of a calf. They brought sacrifices to it and held a celebration in honor of what their hands had made. [42] But God turned away and gave them over to the worship of the heavenly bodies. This agrees with what is written in the book of the prophets: "'Did you bring me sacrifices and offerings forty years in the desert, O house of Israel? [43] You have lifted up the shrine of Molech and the star of your god Rephan, the idols you made to worship. Therefore I will send you into exile' beyond Babylon. [44] "Our forefathers had the tabernacle of the Testimony with them in the desert. It had been made as God directed Moses, according to the pattern he had seen. [45] Having received the tabernacle, our fathers under Joshua brought it with them when they took the land from the nations God drove out before them. It remained in the land until the time of David, [46] who enjoyed God's favor and asked that he might provide a dwelling place for the God of Jacob. [47] But it was Solomon who built

the house for him. [48] "However, the Most High does not live in houses made by men. As the prophet says: [49] "'Heaven is my throne, and the earth is my footstool. What kind of house will you build for me? says the Lord. Or where will my resting place be? [50] Has not my hand made all these things?' [51] "You stiff-necked people, with uncircumcised hearts and ears! You are just like your fathers: You always resist the Holy Spirit! [52] Was there ever a prophet your fathers did not persecute? They even killed those who predicted the coming of the Righteous One. And now you have betrayed and murdered him— [53] you who have received the law that was put into effect through angels but have not obeyed it."

> 1. Why do you think Stephen reminded his listeners of Israel's disobedience to God in the time of Moses?

> 2. What point does Stephen make by bringing up the tabernacle? How does this address the accusations made against him? (Acts 6:13)

> 3. Why do you think Stephen made such direct accusations against his listeners at the end of his sermon? How do you think you would have responded to this sermon if you had been present?

## DAY FOUR READING AND QUESTIONS

[54] When they heard this, they were furious and gnashed their teeth at him. [55] But Stephen, full of the Holy Spirit, looked up to heaven and saw the glory of God, and Jesus standing at the right hand of God. [56] "Look," he said, "I see heaven open and the Son of Man standing at the right hand of God." [57] At this they covered their ears and, yelling at the top of their voices, they all rushed at him, [58] dragged him out of the city and began to stone him. Meanwhile, the witnesses laid their clothes at the feet of a young man named Saul. [59] While they were

stoning him, Stephen prayed, "Lord Jesus, receive my spirit." [60] Then he fell on his knees and cried out, "Lord, do not hold this sin against them." When he had said this, he fell asleep.

1. *Why do you think the crowd responded so violently against Stephen?*

2. *Why do you think God allowed Stephen to see his glory?*

3. *Of what do Stephen's final words remind us? Why does Luke say, "He fell asleep" as Stephen died?*

## DAY FIVE READING AND QUESTIONS

Reread the entire passage (7:1-60)

1. *How did reading the entire passage as one sermon affect you differently than when you read it in four daily readings?*

2. *If given the opportunity of Stephen, how would you retell the story of God? How do you see your life connecting to that story?*

3. *Do you see God as being patient or lacking patience with Israel? How does this influence your thinking about God's dealings with us?*

## MEDITATION

Stephen structured his defense to counter the accusations brought against him—blasphemy against the temple (the holy place), Moses, the law and God himself. Stephen defended himself by retelling the story of Israel, reminding them of how different God's past actions were from what they now expected. This is an important point for us to remember as well. We, like those of Israel, want to believe in a God who promises an easy, successful life in exchange for our faithfulness to him. But there is no such promise in the biblical story. We, too, need to hear Stephen's accurate retelling of the story of God in order to understand the nature of our life in him.

Consider how Stephen dealt with the accusation of blasphemy against Moses. He told the real story of Moses, from God's care for him in infancy to Moses' own desire to lead his people, which ended in failure. One does not lead God's people by one's own initiative. Stephen reminded his listeners that the hero in the story is God, not Moses. Moses led because God chose him to lead. But even with a leader as great as Moses, what did Israel do? They built a calf to worship, and later turned fully to idolatry, so God allowed them to suffer the consequences of their sin. Were these not the ones, then, who were truly guilty of blasphemy against Moses?

Stephen then turned his attention toward the charge of blasphemy against the "holy place" or the temple. He reminded Israel it was not a temple but the tabernacle God instructed them to build. Stephen insinuates that the whole idea of building the temple was man's initiative, not God's. They had placed their faith in a building God had not instructed them to build. Could God be contained in a building or controlled by it? Stephen was not blaspheming the temple, but rather reminding them of what God truly wanted through worship—their hearts.

Stephen told the story of a God who acted according to his promises while his people constantly turned away from him. What prophet had they not killed? At the end of his sermon, Stephen turned on his accusers and revealed they were acting just as Israel always had—in disobedience. Now the Messiah had come, and God's people had killed even him! As those before them, they too resisted the Holy Spirit. Rather than repenting, the crowd allowed their hearts to harden once again, and with great fury charged Stephen, carrying him out of the city and stoning him to death. Even in his death, Stephen embodied Jesus, asking God not to hold this sin against his murderers.

We must not let this sermon leave us unaffected. It calls us to ask, "Have we submitted to the will of God? Do we really know his story?" Or might we be the ones who like Stephen's accusers have refused to hear God's voice and revised his story to fit what we want out of life? Have we created structures of religion (like the temple) which allow us to limit our submission to God to a few rituals a week? Are we the faithful servants whom God will use to deliver others, even if it costs us our lives? Or are we part of the crowd of antagonists who attempt to defeat God's purposes? Remember, not all of the opposition in these stories was intentionally working against God. Some were simply looking out for themselves (Joseph's brothers, for example). But they were not looking to God for direction. Joseph, in contrast, acknowledged the need for a rescuer, and God responded mightily. Stephen's sermon challenges us to find who we are in God's redemptive narrative. There is no middle ground.

"Dear God, may we seek your will in all things. Turn us away from self-will."

# THE GOOD NEWS TO SAMARIA

## (ACTS 8:1-25)

## DAY ONE READING AND QUESTIONS

¹ And Saul was there, giving approval to his death. On that day, a great persecution broke out against the church at Jerusalem, and all except the apostles were scattered throughout Judea and Samaria. ² Godly men buried Stephen and mourned deeply for him. ³ But Saul began to destroy the church. Going from house to house, he dragged off men and women and put them in prison. ⁴ Those who had been scattered preached the word wherever they went. ⁵ Philip went down to a city in Samaria and proclaimed the Christ there. ⁶ When the crowds heard Philip and saw the miraculous signs he did, they all paid close attention to what he said. ⁷ With shrieks, evil spirits came out of many, and many paralytics and cripples were healed. ⁸ So there was great joy in that city.

1. *Why do you think Stephen's speech caused such turmoil throughout the city?*

2. *Why is it significant that those who where scattered continued to preach the word? What does this tell us about their courage and their faith?*

3. *Why was there great joy in the Samaritan city while there was persecution and arrests in Jerusalem?*

## DAY TWO READING AND QUESTIONS

[9] Now for some time a man named Simon had practiced sorcery in the city and amazed all the people of Samaria. He boasted that he was someone great, [10] and all the people, both high and low, gave him their attention and exclaimed, "This man is the divine power known as the Great Power." [11] They followed him because he had amazed them for a long time with his magic. [12] But when they believed Philip as he preached the good news of the kingdom of God and the name of Jesus Christ, they were baptized, both men and women.

*1. What do you think was the source of Simon's sorcery power?*

*2. What was the content of Philip's preaching?*

*3. Why do you think the Samaritans believed Philip and were baptized? Why does Luke mention both men and women obeyed?*

## DAY THREE READING AND QUESTIONS

[13] Simon himself believed and was baptized. And he followed Philip everywhere, astonished by the great signs and miracles he saw. [14] When the apostles in Jerusalem heard that Samaria had accepted the word of God, they sent Peter and John to them. [15] When they arrived, they prayed for them that they might receive the Holy Spirit, [16] because the Holy Spirit had not yet come upon any of them; they had simply been baptized into the name of the Lord Jesus. [17] Then Peter and John placed their hands on them, and they received the Holy Spirit.

*1. What do you think Simon believed when the text says he "believed and was baptized"?*

*2. What does Simon's astonishment tell you about his own "great power?"*

*3. Why do you think the Holy Spirit played such a major role in Luke's account of the beginnings of the church? What do you think Luke would teach us about the Holy Spirit's role in today's church?*

## DAY FOUR READING AND QUESTIONS

[18] When Simon saw that the Spirit was given at the laying on of the apostles' hands, he offered them money [19] and said, "Give me also this ability so that everyone on whom I lay my hands may receive the Holy Spirit." [20] Peter answered: "May your money perish with you, because you thought you could buy the gift of God with money! [21] You have no part or share in this ministry, because your heart is not right before God. [22] Repent of this wickedness and pray to the Lord. Perhaps he will forgive you for having such a thought in your heart. [23] For I see that you are full of bitterness and captive to sin." [24] Then Simon answered, "Pray to the Lord for me so that nothing you have said may happen to me." [25] When they had testified and proclaimed the word of the Lord, Peter and John returned to Jerusalem, preaching the gospel in many Samaritan villages.

*1. Why did Simon want the power of the apostles?*

*2. Whose gift, according to Peter, was the Holy Spirit? What does this suggest about Peter's role in the giving of the Holy Spirit?*

*3. Why did Peter say that Simon was full of bitterness and captive to sin? What did his greed have to do with bitterness?*

*4. Have you ever felt envious toward a brother or sister who had a particular gift? What should we do when we have such thoughts?*

## DAY FIVE READING AND QUESTIONS

Reread the entire passage (Acts 8:1-25)

*1. If someone were hunting you down to throw you into prison, would you have the courage to preach the good news of Jesus and his kingdom?*

*2. Have you ever witnessed the joy of one giving their life to Jesus who previously had not known the good news of his kingdom? How can we recapture that joy in our churches?*

*3. What motivated Simon to obey the gospel? What do you think Luke wants us to learn from the Simon episode?*

# MEDITATION

The story of the church in Acts is one of constant expansion, not just in numbers, but in reaching into new people groups. Social, national, and ethnic barriers began to fall. The Holy Spirit broke the language barrier on Pentecost. Now serious cultural barriers begin to fall as the kingdom of God expands into the world. God's care and love for all the nations, as seen in the prophets, is becoming a reality. What caused such expansion? The persecution that followed Stephen's death did not put out the flames of passion for Jesus Christ;

it spread the fire of the gospel to new nations.

Luke's narrative follows Philip (one of the seven) to Samaria—not as an isolated case, but as one example of the many scattered who preached wherever they went. We continue to see the astonishing and sometimes puzzling work of the Holy Spirit. The Spirit led Stephen to preach boldly, ending in his death, but the Spirit would lead Philip to lands and peoples not yet reached with the gospel. The Spirit leads where he wills. The biblical story reminds us to leave the outcomes to him.

Philip's preaching in Samaria was joyously received. People were listening, watching, and opening their hearts to the word. Evil spirits were cast out, healings were celebrated—in fact, the whole city broke out in joy. One cannot help but notice the difference between Jerusalem and Samaria. In one, there was persecution, anger and hard hearts. In the other, there was joy and celebration. The message and marvels were the same. But some refused to hear the good news, pre-ferring the comfort of what they had always known. Again, Luke would have us ask ourselves, "Who would we be in this story?"

What do we do with the story of Simon? It reveals to us one deeply impacted by the power of the gospel, but who responds to it out of self-interest. His former powers of sorcery were nothing in comparison to the power of Philip. Now, no one baptized by Philip had received the Holy Spirit. The conversion of the Samaritans was such a cultural barrier, it was necessary to demonstrate it was indeed of God by having Peter and John come from Jerusalem and lay their hands on these new believers. When Simon saw Peter and John give others the gift of the Holy Spirit, this was too much for egotistic Simon to bear. He saw a magnificent and profitable capability. Simon quickly let Peter know he would pay a great amount of money if Peter would give him this ability.

Peter's answer was pointed. The attempt to use money coercively once again appears in the story. God's gifts were not for sale. Simon's request exposed a heart full of bitterness and a life that was captive to sin. When confronted by Peter, Simon quickly repented and asked for forgiveness.

Let's ask ourselves, "Could it be that I have some of Simon in me? Am I giving up my personal 'great power' but desiring ultimately to be the focus of others' admiration?" We need to fall on our knees and ask God for forgiveness. And the word of God will continue to spread as we turn away from self-worship and give ourselves totally to the One who will give us all the attention we need.

"Generous Lord, open my eyes to my own self-interests, so that I might serve you with a pure heart."

# THE GOOD NEWS EMBRACED BY AN ETHIOPIAN
## (ACTS 8:26-40)

### DAY ONE READING AND QUESTIONS

²⁶ Now an angel of the Lord said to Philip, "Go south to the road—the desert road—that goes down from Jerusalem to Gaza." ²⁷ So he started out, and on his way he met an Ethiopian eunuch, an important official in charge of all the treasury of Candace, queen of the Ethiopians. This man had gone to Jerusalem to worship, ²⁸ and on his way home was sitting in his chariot reading the book of Isaiah the prophet.

*1. What made Philip so useful for the Lord's purposes?*

*2. What was the Ethiopian's job and why had he been to Jerusalem?*

*3. Of all those who had traveled to Jerusalem to worship, why do you think the Lord chose the Ethiopian to hear the good news of Jesus?*

## DAY TWO READING AND QUESTIONS

[29] The Spirit told Philip, "Go to that chariot and stay near it." [30] Then Philip ran up to the chariot and heard the man reading Isaiah the prophet. "Do you understand what you are reading?" Philip asked. [31] "How can I," he said, "unless someone explains it to me?" So he invited Philip to come up and sit with him. [32] The eunuch was reading this passage of Scripture: "He was led like a sheep to the slaughter, and as a lamb before the shearer is silent, so he did not open his mouth. [33] In his humiliation he was deprived of justice. Who can speak of his descendants? For his life was taken from the earth." [34] The eunuch asked Philip, "Tell me, please, who is the prophet talking about, himself or someone else?"

*1. What does this event tell us about the work of the Holy Spirit?*

*2. Why do you think the Ethiopian invited Philip into his chariot?*

*3. If someone asked you the question asked by the Ethiopian (v. 34), how would you answer?*

## DAY THREE READING AND QUESTIONS

[35] Then Philip began with that very passage of Scripture and told him the good news about Jesus. [36] As they traveled along the road,

they came to some water and the eunuch said, "Look, here is water. Why shouldn't I be baptized?" [37] NOTE: (some late manuscripts add 37 Philip said "If you believe with all your heart, you may." The eunuch answered, "I believe that Jesus Christ is the Son of God.")

    *1. What was the good news about Jesus that Philip told the Ethiopian?*

    *2. Why do you think baptism came to the Ethiopian's mind when he saw water?*

    *3. Does the addition of verse 37 add anything to this story? If it was added by later copiers (as it most likely was), why do you think it was added?*

## DAY FOUR READING AND QUESTIONS

[38] And he gave orders to stop the chariot. Then both Philip and the eunuch went down into the water and Philip baptized him. [39] When they came up out of the water, the Spirit of the Lord suddenly took Philip away, and the eunuch did not see him again, but went on his way rejoicing. [40] Philip, however, appeared at Azotus and traveled about, preaching the gospel in all the towns until he reached Caesarea.

    *1. What was there in Philip's presentation of the good news that led the Ethiopian to want new life?*

    *2. What do you think the Ethiopian did with his newly found faith in Jesus?*

    *3. What have you done to spread the good news of Jesus to those with whom you interact on a daily basis?*

## DAY FIVE READING AND QUESTIONS

Reread the entire passage (Acts 8:26-40)

1. *How can we encourage one another to have the willingness of Philip to follow the lead of God's Spirit?*

2. *Do you intentionally make yourself available to the Holy Spirit to "walk beside" seekers of truth who do not know Jesus? Do we intently listen to the difficulties of others' lives so that we might offer them a word of encouragement from the Lord?*

3. *Have you ever led one to faith? Relive the joy of that moment and thank God for using you in that way.*

# MEDITATION

Read Isaiah 53-56:5. Try to imagine yourself as the Ethiopian official attempting to understand the message. Is there anything in those verses that would be of meaning? What led a struggling African noble to request baptism?

Eunuchs could not participate in temple worship. Nonetheless, he had committed himself to a long and expensive pilgrimage to Jerusalem. He shows his deep devotion by investing in a scroll that included Isaiah—a costly purchase. Can you imagine his anticipation in reading the text as he traveled home? However, he found great difficulty in understanding the prophecy of a suffering servant. Philip walked beside his chariot and heard him reading the Isaiah text. "Do you understand?" Philip asked. Thus began the conversation that would radically change the Ethiopian's life.

As they continued to read the scroll, they would have read Isaiah 56:3-4. The message became amazingly personal. According to Isaiah's prophecy, eunuchs were no longer excluded from full participation in worship in God's kingdom! All things are new! In the time of Messiah, one could claim new life. New life!

This is a marvelous text to lead us to think about how we approach telling others about Jesus. Acts provides us with a wealth of wonderful conversion stories. These stories instruct us about the work of the Spirit in the process of conversion. The Spirit led Philip to the Ethiopian. Would it not be strange if the Spirit did not continue to work in this way? Maybe we don't hear a voice guiding us to a specific road, but how many times have you found yourself in just the right place and time to introduce someone to the God they seek? We need to tune our ears and hearts to hear the confused cries of those around us.

In my mission experience, nearly every story of conversion I have heard has involved God arranging meetings of seekers with "Philips." Are we willing to be used in such a way? You may not feel adequately prepared for such a task. But you are. You have experienced salvation in Christ. The Holy Spirit dwells in you. You have a story to tell. God has chosen you as an interpreter of his word of life for the world.

I cannot hear the story of Philip and the Ethiopian without reflecting on an event in my life. A good friend was very confused and disillusioned about life. We walked together often—I would try to convince him God's offer for life was the answer he sought. After one such afternoon together, during which we constantly talked about God and his purpose for our lives, we crossed a beautiful stream on our drive home. My friend asked, "Is there anything that would keep me from starting new life right here?" I stopped the car and together we walked into that flowing stream, and I buried my friend's confusion about life and watched the Lord make everything new and exciting for him. I will never forget him lifting me in the air and shouting, "I'm clean, I'm clean. Life starts for me today." This experience has taken on even deeper meaning as I write, because recently my good brother unexpectedly left this life much too soon.

Friends, we are invited to participate in God's redemptive story by walking beside the struggling and providing answers only God can give—and we are the chosen vessel through whom he speaks to those around us. There is no better use of life than this.

"Gracious Lord, open my ears to hear the confusion of those beside whom I walk. May I clearly see the many opportunities you give me daily to share the peace that comes only from you."

# THE CALLING OF SAUL
## (ACTS 9:1-31)

### DAY ONE READING AND QUESTIONS

[1] Meanwhile, Saul was still breathing out murderous threats against the Lord's disciples. He went to the high priest [2] and asked him for letters to the synagogues in Damascus, so that if he found any there who belonged to the Way, whether men or women, he might take them as prisoners to Jerusalem. [3] As he neared Damascus on his journey, suddenly a light from heaven flashed around him. [4] He fell to the ground and heard a voice say to him, "Saul, Saul, why do you persecute me?" [5] "Who are you, Lord?" Saul asked. "I am Jesus, whom you are persecuting," he replied. [6] "Now get up and go into the city, and you will be told what you must do." [7] The men traveling with Saul stood there speechless; they heard the sound but did not see anyone. [8]

Saul got up from the ground, but when he opened his eyes he could see nothing. So they led him by the hand into Damascus. ⁹ For three days he was blind, and did not eat or drink anything.

*1. What is the name by which Saul knew the early church? Would this be a good description for the church today? Why or why not?*

*2. What do you think Saul felt in his heart when he heard the voice identify itself as that of Jesus?*

*3. If Jesus would speak to you today, what do you think would be his greatest concern pertaining to your life?*

## DAY TWO READING AND QUESTIONS

¹⁰ In Damascus there was a disciple named Ananias. The Lord called to him in a vision, "Ananias!" "Yes, Lord," he answered. ¹¹ The Lord told him, "Go to the house of Judas on Straight Street and ask for a man from Tarsus named Saul, for he is praying. ¹² In a vision he has seen a man named Ananias come and place his hands on him to restore his sight." ¹³ "Lord," Ananias answered, "I have heard many reports about this man and all the harm he has done to your saints in Jerusalem. ¹⁴And he has come here with authority from the chief priests to arrest all who call on your name." ¹⁵ But the Lord said to Ananias, "Go! This man is my chosen instrument to carry my name before the Gentiles and their kings and before the people of Israel. ¹⁶ I will show him how much he must suffer for my name." ¹⁷ Then Ananias went to the house and entered it. Placing his hands on Saul, he said, "Brother Saul, the Lord— Jesus, who appeared to you on the road as you were coming here— has sent me so that you may see again and be filled with the Holy Spirit." ¹⁸ Immediately, something

like scales fell from Saul's eyes, and he could see again. He got up and was baptized, [19] and after taking some food, he regained his strength. Saul spent several days with the disciples in Damascus.

1. *While Saul was not eating or drinking anything, what was he doing?*

2. *What did the Lord reveal to Saul as he prayed?*

3. *What was the Lord's plan for Saul?*

4. *Do you think the Lord has specific plans for you? What do you think they are?*

## DAY THREE READING AND QUESTIONS

[20] At once he began to preach in the synagogues that Jesus is the Son of God. [21] All those who heard him were astonished and asked, "Isn't he the man who raised havoc in Jerusalem among those who call on this name? And hasn't he come here to take them as prisoners to the chief priests?" [22] Yet Saul grew more and more powerful and baffled the Jews living in Damascus by proving that Jesus is the Christ. [23] After many days had gone by, the Jews conspired to kill him, [24] but Saul learned of their plan. Day and night they kept close watch on the city gates in order to kill him. [25] But his followers took him by night and lowered him in a basket through an opening in the wall.

1. *What was the content of Saul's preaching?*

2. *What was Saul able to prove?*

3. *Why do you think the Jews were so ready to kill those who proclaimed Jesus as Christ or Messiah? Why was this message so threatening?*

## DAY FOUR READING AND QUESTIONS

[26] When he came to Jerusalem, he tried to join the disciples, but they were all afraid of him, not believing that he really was a disciple. [27] But Barnabas took him and brought him to the apostles. He told them how Saul on his journey had seen the Lord and that the Lord had spoken to him, and how in Damascus he had preached fearlessly in the name of Jesus. [28] So Saul stayed with them and moved about freely in Jerusalem, speaking boldly in the name of the Lord. [29] He talked and debated with the Grecian Jews, but they tried to kill him. [30] When the brothers learned of this, they took him down to Caesarea and sent him off to Tarsus. [31] Then the church throughout Judea, Galilee and Samaria enjoyed a time of peace. It was strengthened; and encouraged by the Holy Spirit, it grew in numbers, living in the fear of the Lord.

*1. After this reading, what more do we know of Barnabas? Do you know anyone with similar qualities? If so, how do you feel when around him/her?*

*2. How could the church enjoy a time of peace and yet live in the fear of the Lord? How would you describe this "fear of the Lord"?*

*3. Is it possible for today's church to experience again the summary statement at the end of verse 31? If so, how can we help make this happen?*

## DAY FIVE READING AND QUESTIONS

Reread the entire passage (Acts 9:1-31)

*1. Have you gained any new insights into Paul's conversion? If so, what are they?*

*2. Write down your own story of conversion. Do you remember the joy of new birth?*

*3. What scales have you had in your eyes that have prevented you from seeing life as God would have you see it?*

# MEDITATION

The Lord's miraculous intervention in Paul's conversion is unlike any other story in God's history with humanity (I choose to call Saul "Paul" since this is the name we use most often to identify him). Some have compared this to Moses' "burning bush" experience. But Moses was not intentionally pursuing anything as a shepherd in Midian—he was simply escaping harm and surviving. Paul, unlike Moses, was zealous to do the will of God. However, he was actually working directly against God's purposes. Paul was a leader in the movement to eradicate Jerusalem of any followers of Jesus, and apparently had done so much damage to the church there that he was looking for new challenges. So he headed to Damascus to pursue Christians there. It was during this journey that God radically redirected Paul's life.

What can we learn from Paul's conversion story? God is a God of great mercy, is he not? Though Paul was persecuting the body of Jesus Christ (the church), God called him to new life in his kingdom. After three days of contemplating the darkness of his life, Paul's sight was restored. He saw a new world! Luke wants us to see a direct connection between the giving of the Holy Spirit and Paul's sight being restored. This is what the Holy Spirit does. He gives us new eyes with which to see our world. No matter where you have been or what you have done, God is calling you to new life. He will abundantly forgive and give you new life.

After Paul's baptism, he was more zealous to proclaim the good news in Jesus than his former zeal to defeat it. Wouldn't it have been great to hear his preaching in Damascus? Can you imagine being in the community that once viewed Paul's arrival with great fear, now hearing him proclaim the good news with great boldness? How encouraging to realize the power of the gospel to change lives! God is actively seeking those whom we would never consider candidates for conversion.

At the end of this exciting story of conversion, Luke gives us a summary of the church's work to that point. The church throughout the region enjoyed a time of peace. "It was strengthened; and encouraged by the Holy Spirit, it grew in numbers, living in the fear of the Lord." We live in a time of relative peace. Of course, we are all concerned about the violence present in our world. But we are free to pursue God. How do we use that peace? Are we strengthened, encouraged by the Holy Spirit, growing in numbers and living in the awareness of God's magnificent power and grace? If we are not, why is this so? Is God less present? We know this is not true. Might it be, then, that we are we so distracted by our own busy lives we fail to acknowledge our need for God?

"Gracious Lord, may we never take for granted our desperate need for you."

# PETER EMBODIES JESUS
## (ACTS 9:32-42)

## DAY ONE READING AND QUESTIONS

[32] As Peter traveled about the country, he went to visit the saints in Lydda. [33] There he found a man named Aeneas, a paralytic who had been bedridden for eight years. [34] "Aeneas," Peter said to him, "Jesus Christ heals you. Get up and take care of your mat." Immediately Aeneas got up.

*1. Of what event in the life of Jesus does this remind you?*

*2. What did Peter say as he healed Aeneas? Why is this significant?*

*3. If you were to identify a spiritual illness of which you need to be cured, what would it be? Have you asked God for healing?*

## DAY TWO READING AND QUESTIONS

[36] In Joppa there was a disciple named Tabitha (which, when translated, is Dorcas), who was always doing good and helping the poor. [37] About that time she became sick and died, and her body was washed and placed in an upstairs room. [38] Lydda was near Joppa; so when the disciples heard that Peter was in Lydda, they sent two men to him and urged him, "Please come at once!"

*1. What do we know of Tabitha or Dorcas?*

*2. Why do you think they sent for Peter?*

*3. When you read about Dorcas, does she remind you of anyone in your life? If so, describe that person.*

## DAY THREE READING AND QUESTIONS

[39] Peter went with them, and when he arrived he was taken upstairs to the room. All the widows stood around him, crying and showing him the robes and other clothing that Dorcas had made while she was still with them. [40] Peter sent them all out of the room; then he got down on his knees and prayed. Turning toward the dead woman, he said, "Tabitha, get up." She opened her eyes, and seeing Peter she sat up.

*1. If you were to die, what would people show others that you had done for them?*

*2. Who was standing around Peter, and why is this significant?*

*3. Why do you think Peter sent everyone out of the room?*

## DAY FOUR READING AND QUESTIONS

[41] He took her by the hand and helped her to her feet. Then he called the believers and the widows and presented her to them alive. [42] This became known all over Joppa, and many people believed in the Lord.

*1. What do you see in all these miracles concerning the state of an individual immediately after healing? Why is this so impressive?*

*2. What did Peter do before he raised Dorcas from the dead? Why is this significant?*

*3. Why would such a miracle cause people to believe in the Lord instead of Peter? What does this tell you about Peter's work?*

## DAY FIVE READING AND QUESTIONS

Reread the entire passage (Acts 9:32-42)

*1. In what way can we help the lame to walk, and give life to the dead?*

*2. Do your good works help people believe in Jesus? Why or why not?*

*3. How can we more effectively turn people toward Jesus through our ministry efforts?*

## MEDITATION

Apparently, Peter was constantly on the move. He was not running from authorities. He was on a mission. One cannot help but see the image of Jesus in Peter. In fact, whatever Peter did, he did in the name of Jesus Christ. We remember Jesus' words in the gospel of John, "Apart from me, you can do nothing." One of the most basic teachings of Jesus was our need to abide in him intentionally. As Jesus abided in the Father, and did nothing apart from him, so we are to live in him. Luke wants us to see what that life is like through the early heroes of faith.

Imagine the joy that the healing of Aeneas must have brought.

For eight years he had been confined to his bed. In a moment, he was completely healed. The amazing thing about this healing is not just the removal of the paralytic condition, but the immediate ability to walk—with the strength to pick up his mat! God granted him strength, coordination, balance—all of this was immediate. Find someone involved in physical therapy and ask them how long it would take to recover muscle strength in a patient whose body had atrophied for eight years. Ask how long it would take to teach balance and eye foot coordination. Who could doubt that God was involved in such a miracle? What Peter was preaching about God's kingdom and his Messiah had to be true.

Luke clearly wants us to see Jesus in Peter's actions. With Aeneas, we remember the paralytic let down through the roof in front of Jesus. The story of Tabitha (Dorcas) is a close parallel to Jesus' raising of Jairus' daughter. The child's body was in an upper room, so was Dorcas.' People were mourning the child's death as the widows were mourning Dorcas.' Jesus sent them out of the room—as did Peter. Jesus called to her, "Talitha, cum" ("my child, get up!"). Here Peter calls out, "Tabitha, cum" ("Dorcas, get up"). The ministry of Jesus continues through his disciples. The lame walk, the dead receive life. Indeed, the Messianic Age, the kingdom of God, has come. Jesus is alive in his church.

We should not miss the opportunity to meditate on the kind and generous life of Dorcas. She was "always doing good and helping the poor." As Peter climbed the stairs to the room containing Dorcas' body, mourning widows, who wanted Peter to see the clothing Dorcas had made for them, surrounded him. This scene challenges each of us to think about the contribution we are making to those in need. If we died today, what would be the gifts we have given to those in need? Would our friends characterize us as one "always doing good and helping the poor?" What, in the actions of our lives, has ultimate value?

"Lord, by what I say and do may I call to mind the life of Jesus to those around me."

# CORNELIUS HEARS THE GOOD NEWS
## (ACTS 10:1-43)

### DAY ONE READING AND QUESTIONS

[1] At Caesarea there was a man named Cornelius, a centurion in what was known as the Italian Regiment. [2] He and all his family were devout and God-fearing; he gave generously to those in need and prayed to God regularly. [3] One day at about three in the afternoon he had a vision. He distinctly saw an angel of God, who came to him and said, "Cornelius!" [4] Cornelius stared at him in fear. "What is it, Lord?" he asked. The angel answered, "Your prayers and gifts to the poor have come up as a memorial offering before God. [5] Now send men to Joppa to bring back a man named Simon who is called Peter. [6] He is staying with Simon the tanner, whose house is by the sea." [7] When the angel who spoke to him had gone, Cornelius called two of his servants and a devout soldier who was one of his attendants. [8] He told them everything that had happened and sent them to Joppa.

1. *What do we know of Cornelius according to this reading?*

2. *Why do you think God chose Cornelius to be the first Gentile to hear the good news?*

3. *Does his telling of his vision to a military aid and two servants tell us anything about Cornelius and his relationship to those under his command?*

## DAY TWO READING AND QUESTIONS

[9] About noon the following day as they were on their journey and approaching the city, Peter went up on the roof to pray. [10] He became hungry and wanted something to eat, and while the meal was being prepared, he fell into a trance. [11] He saw heaven opened and something like a large sheet being let down to earth by its four corners. [12] It contained all kinds of four-footed animals, as well as reptiles of the earth and birds of the air. [13] Then a voice told him, "Get up, Peter. Kill and eat." [14] "Surely not, Lord!" Peter replied. "I have never eaten anything impure or unclean." [15] The voice spoke to him a second time, "Do not call anything impure that God has made clean." [16] This happened three times, and immediately the sheet was taken back to heaven. [17] While Peter was wondering about the meaning of the vision, the men sent by Cornelius found out where Simon's house was and stopped at the gate. [18] They called out, asking if Simon who was known as Peter was staying there. [19] While Peter was still thinking about the vision, the Spirit said to him, "Simon, three men are looking for you. [20] So get up and go downstairs. Do not hesitate to go with them, for I have sent them." [21] Peter went down and said to the men, "I'm the one you're looking for. Why have you come?" [22] The men replied, "We have come from Cornelius the centurion. He is a righteous and God-fearing man, who is respected by all the Jewish people. A holy angel told him to have you come to his house so that he could hear what you have to say." [23] Then Peter invited the men into the house to be his guests. The next day Peter started out with them, and some of the brothers from Joppa went along.

*1. Why did Peter refuse to obey the voice of the Lord?*

*2. Why was Peter so confused by the vision, especially after the same thing happened three times?*

*3. Is there anything in your spiritual development where you have had to change your thinking? What ultimately caused you to change?*

## DAY THREE READING AND QUESTIONS

[24] The following day he arrived in Caesarea. Cornelius was expecting them and had called together his relatives and close friends. [25] As Peter entered the house, Cornelius met him and fell at his feet in reverence. [26] But Peter made him get up. "Stand up," he said, "I am only a man myself." [27] Talking with him, Peter went inside and found a large gathering of people. [28] He said to them: "You are well aware that it is against our law for a Jew to associate with a Gentile or visit him. But God has shown me that I should not call any man impure or unclean. [29] So when I was sent for, I came without raising any objection. May I ask why you sent for me?" [30] Cornelius answered: "Four days ago I was in my house praying at this hour, at three in the afternoon. Suddenly a man in shining clothes stood before me [31] and said, 'Cornelius, God has heard your prayer and remembered your gifts to the poor. [32] Send to Joppa for Simon who is called Peter. He is a guest in the home of Simon the tanner, who lives by the sea.' [33] So I sent for you immediately, and it was good of you to come. Now we are all here in the presence of God to listen to everything the Lord has commanded you to tell us."

*1. Why do you think Cornelius invited his relatives and close friends to hear what Peter had to say?*

*2. What had Peter understood his vision to mean?*

*3. If God was responding to Cornelius' prayers by sending Peter to speak, what might we guess was Cornelius' petition to the Lord?*

## DAY FOUR READING AND QUESTIONS

[34] Then Peter began to speak: "I now realize how true it is that God does not show favoritism [35] but accepts men from every nation who fear him and do what is right. [36] You know the message God sent to the people of Israel, telling the good news of peace through Jesus Christ, who is Lord of all. [37] You know what has happened throughout Judea, beginning in Galilee after the baptism that John preached—[38]how God anointed Jesus of Nazareth with the Holy Spirit and power, and how he went around doing good and healing all who were under the power of the devil, because God was with him. [39] "We are witnesses of everything he did in the country of the Jews and in Jerusalem. They killed him by hanging him on a tree, [40] but God raised him from the dead on the third day and caused him to be seen. [41] He was not seen by all the people, but by witnesses whom God had already chosen—by us who ate and drank with him after he rose from the dead. [42] He commanded us to preach to the people and to testify that he is the one whom God appointed as judge of the living and the dead. [43] All the prophets testify about him that everyone who believes in him receives forgiveness of sins through his name."

*1. About what did Peter assume all who were listening had heard?*

*2. How did Peter summarize Jesus' life?*

*3. Why did Peter bring up the testimony of the prophets? Why would that be important to Gentiles?*

## DAY FIVE READING AND QUESTIONS

Reread the entire passage (Acts 10:1-43)

*1. What new understandings of God have you experienced which significantly changed your view of the world?*

*2. What might we learn from Peter in this story?*

*3. What might we learn from Cornelius in this story?*

# MEDITATION

Most Roman soldiers, particularly centurions, used their power and authority in coercive ways for personal gain. Cornelius, however, was different. He was a devout man—known as one who gave generously and prayed regularly. What better candidate could there have been among Gentiles to receive the first invitation into God's kingdom? It was for these reasons that God sought him out. God was working to arrange a special meeting—and he had to work on both ends of this one.

We learn important things from both Peter and Cornelius' part in the story. Peter learns that the work of Christ has significantly altered some former restrictions concerning what is clean and unclean. From Peter's part in the story, we are called to ask some difficult questions of ourselves. "What or who do I regard as 'untouchable' that God wants me to reach with the gospel?" "Whom have I ignored that God would have me bring to repentance?" Cornelius experiences an amazing intervention of God in his life in response to his prayer. When he realizes what God has done, he invites all his household and friends to share in his blessing. Cornelius reminds us of the joy of salvation and the importance of seeking God.

I doubt the difficulty of this moment for Peter could be overstated. There are few analogies in our modern culture comparable to the deep divide between the Jews and Gentiles. Peter actually seems proud of himself as he enters the house of Cornelius and says, "God has shown me not to call you profane or unclean. He has revealed to me that I am allowed to enter your house without defiling myself." We cringe at this opening statement. How could Peter say such an offensive thing? But Cornelius understood the profound nature of the concession Peter was making. This was indeed a significant moment in salvation history.

Peter then delivers a powerful exposition of the gospel. Note that he presumes they know about Jesus—because they certainly did. Throughout Luke/Acts, Luke wants Theophilus to know these things didn't happen in some obscure little village. Everyone knew these events. Peter, speaking to those gathered in Cornelius' house, proclaims Jesus Christ as Lord of all. He tells them that the prophets spoke of this great event. This shows to what extent Cornelius had taught his household and friends of God's word—they were familiar with the prophets. Peter's message hit the intended target. The message moved them deeply.

The conversion stories throughout Acts are all God's work. The triune God—the Father, the Son, and the Holy Spirit—is working to invite all into the kingdom. The purpose of the church, and the faithful believers throughout Acts, is to be God's agents in his work of salvation. Today as then, God breaks down our misconceptions, works in the hearts of the unbeliever, and arranges the meeting. Are our hearts and minds attuned to the Lord so that we are available at his calling?

"Lord of all, open our minds and hearts to all those who are seeking you. May we never exclude a person from your grace because of our inappropriate judgment."

# GENTILES RECEIVE THE HOLY SPIRIT
## (ACTS 10:44-11:18)

### DAY ONE READING AND QUESTIONS

[44] While Peter was still speaking these words, the Holy Spirit came on all who heard the message. [45] The circumcised believers who had come with Peter were astonished that the gift of the Holy Spirit had been poured out even on the Gentiles. [46] For they heard them speaking in tongues and praising God. Then Peter said, [47] "Can anyone keep these people from being baptized with water? They have received the Holy Spirit just as we have." [48] So he ordered that they be baptized in the name of Jesus Christ. Then they asked Peter to stay with them for a few days.

*1. Why do you think the Holy Spirit came upon all who heard before they asked?*

*2. How did this affect the believing Jews who were present?*

*3. If you had been one of the Gentiles converted in this story, what questions would you have asked Peter in the days that followed?*

## DAY TWO READING AND QUESTIONS

¹ The apostles and the brothers throughout Judea heard that the Gentiles also had received the word of God. ² So when Peter went up to Jerusalem, the circumcised believers criticized him ³ and said, "You went into the house of uncircumcised men and ate with them." ⁴ Peter began and explained everything to them precisely as it had happened: ⁵ "I was in the city of Joppa praying, and in a trance I saw a vision. I saw something like a large sheet being let down from heaven by its four corners, and it came down to where I was.

*1. Why did the Jews in Jerusalem greet Peter with criticism?*

*2. Why do you think Luke has Peter repeat the story with such detail?*

*3. Can you think of a time when you felt led by the Lord to do some-thing that produced criticism? What can we learn from Peter on how to confront such a situation?*

## DAY THREE READING AND QUESTIONS

⁶ I looked into it and saw four-footed animals of the earth, wild beasts, reptiles, and birds of the air. ⁷ Then I heard a voice telling me, 'Get up, Peter. Kill and eat.' ⁸ "I replied, 'Surely not, Lord! Nothing impure or unclean has ever entered my mouth.' ⁹ "The voice spoke from heaven a second time, 'Do not call anything impure that God has made clean.' ¹⁰ This happened three times, and then it was all pulled up to heaven again.

*1. Why is it significant that Peter had the same vision three times?*

*2. How could God make something "clean" that had once been "unclean"?*

*3. How do we develop the discernment to know a message is clearly from the Lord?*

## DAY FOUR READING AND QUESTIONS

[11] "Right then three men who had been sent to me from Caesarea stopped at the house where I was staying. [12] The Spirit told me to have no hesitation about going with them. These six brothers also went with me, and we entered the man's house. [13] He told us how he had seen an angel appear in his house and say, 'Send to Joppa for Simon who is called Peter. [14] He will bring you a message through which you and all your household will be saved.' [15] "As I began to speak, the Holy Spirit came on them as he had come on us at the beginning. [16] Then I remembered what the Lord had said: 'John baptized with water, but you will be baptized with the Holy Spirit.' [17] So if God gave them the same gift as he gave us, who believed in the Lord Jesus Christ, who was I to think that I could oppose God?" [18] When they heard this, they had no further objections and praised God, saying, "So then, God has granted even the Gentiles repentance unto life."

*1. Why was it important that Peter had six other Jewish believers with him?*

*2. What reasoning did Peter use to justify his association with the Gentiles of Cornelius' house?*

*3. How did the Jewish believers of Jerusalem characterize God's gift to the Gentiles? Is this the way we characterize our salvation in Jesus?*

## DAY FIVE READING AND QUESTIONS

Reread the entire passage (Acts 10:44-11:18)

*1. What surprises you most about this story?*

*2. What was the objection of the Jewish believers to Peter's actions? What does this tell us about their view of salvation (who did they think it was for)?*

*3. Whom have we disregarded in evangelism?*

## MEDITATION

Imagine how surprised Peter and the other believing Jews must have been when they realized that the Gentiles had received the Holy Spirit! Not only were they Gentiles, but they had not yet been immersed. On Pentecost, Luke tells us the Spirit was given at baptism. In Samaria, the Spirit came only after Peter and John laid their hands on those who had expressed their belief through baptism. What are we to make of all this? How can we know when the Spirit of God is given? Luke's answer would be, "God does what is best in his work of conversion." We want an order of events so that we can understand when and what happens; God wants a change of heart so that those who come to him fully experience kingdom life.

The Jew/Gentile barrier was so immense that God chose to demonstrate his loving acceptance of the Gentiles by giving them the Holy Spirit prior to baptism. If God so clearly affirmed his love for them in this way, who could argue with him? Peter's response is interesting, "How can we withhold baptism if they have the Holy Spirit?"

His question indicates he was at least considering withholding baptism from them, even if they had expressed belief in Jesus as the Christ. After all, they were unclean Gentiles. I wonder if Peter was struggling with this very issue ("What will I do if they believe in Jesus?") while he was teaching them. Not to worry! The Holy Spirit took care of any doubts or misgivings Peter might have had.

This was an important sequence, not only for Peter, but for all of us. It was important for those in Jerusalem who openly disapproved of Peter's actions. They did not criticize him for baptizing the Gentiles, but for eating with them. The sin of breaking the sanctity of table fellowship was apparently the gravest sin in their way of thinking. So Peter tells the story of how God opened his mind to a new way of looking at the world. Three visions with the same message were indisputable. And when Peter told of the Holy Spirit falling on the Gentiles as he spoke, there was no more to be said—except "Well, then, this settles it; God has given even the Gentiles the repentance that leads to life." What a wonderful way of expressing what happens when one accepts Jesus as the Christ! It is turning away from non-life to life—life in the kingdom of God. It was not just repentance in order to believe in a new religion. The Jews, too, would have to repent. They needed to repent of their exclusive view of God's blessings.

Of what should we repent? What keeps us from seeing people as God sees them? God calls and blesses us in order to call others. The blessings of life must not stop with us.

"Dear God, lover of all your creatures, teach me to love as you love."

# CHRISTIAN COMMUNITY IN ANTIOCH

## (ACTS 11:1-30)

### DAY ONE READING AND QUESTIONS

[19] Now those who had been scattered by the persecution in connection with Stephen traveled as far as Phoenicia, Cyprus and Antioch, telling the message only to Jews. [20] Some of them, however, men from Cyprus and Cyrene, went to Antioch and began to speak to Greeks also, telling them the good news about the Lord Jesus. [21] The Lord's hand was with them, and a great number of people believed and turned to the Lord.

*1. Why did the persecuted believers limit their teaching to Jews?*

*2. Why do you think some of them also spoke to the Greeks (Gentiles) about Jesus?*

*3. Why did a great number of people believe? What should this tell us about the content of effective preaching?*

## DAY TWO READING AND QUESTIONS

[22] News of this reached the ears of the church at Jerusalem, and they sent Barnabas to Antioch. [23] When he arrived and saw the evidence of the grace of God, he was glad and encouraged them all to remain true to the Lord with all their hearts. [24] He was a good man, full of the Holy Spirit and faith, and a great number of people were brought to the Lord.

1. *What do you think was the evidence of the grace of God that Barnabas witnessed?*

2. *What was his message to those in Antioch?*

3. *Does this teach us anything about how we should interact as we visit congregations other than our own?*

## DAY THREE READING AND QUESTIONS

[25] Then Barnabas went to Tarsus to look for Saul, [26] and when he found him, he brought him to Antioch. So for a whole year Barnabas and Saul met with the church and taught great numbers of people. The disciples were called Christians first at Antioch.

1. *Why would Barnabas seek out Saul?*

2. *How long did Paul and Barnabas work with the church at Antioch? Does this surprise you?*

3. *Why do you think Luke tells us it was in Antioch that followers of Jesus were first called Christians?*

## DAY FOUR READING AND QUESTIONS

[27] During this time some prophets came down from Jerusalem to Antioch. [28] One of them, named Agabus, stood up and through the Spirit predicted that a severe famine would spread over the entire Roman world. (This happened during the reign of Claudius.) [29] The disciples, each according to his ability, decided to provide help for the brothers living in Judea. [30] This they did, sending their gift to the elders by Barnabas and Saul.

> *1. What does the arrival of the prophets from Jerusalem say about Jerusalem's view of the church in Antioch?*

> *2. What does the willingness of the disciples to help their brothers in Judea demonstrate?*

> *3. When we hear of potential trouble for brothers and sisters in Christ, is our first impulse to help? How can we develop a more spontaneous generosity toward others?*

## DAY FIVE READING AND QUESTIONS

Reread the entire passage (Acts 11:19-29)

> *1. Do you remember the gratitude you first felt when you were baptized in the name of Jesus? How can we keep that sense of thanksgiving alive in our hearts?*

> *2. How can we better teach new converts in Christ? Do you think we do this well enough, or does it need more attention?*

*3. How do you think the brethren in Judea felt when Paul and
Barnabas brought their financial gifts from the Antiochene brethren?*

# MEDITATION

While persecution was thought to be a way of destroying this
"new cult" (as its enemies saw it), instead it acted as an accelerant to
the fire of the kingdom. Some of those who fled Jerusalem spread out
to far away places, but they were not discouraged or dissuaded from
their belief in Jesus as Lord. Everywhere they went they proclaimed
the good news of the kingdom of God. God blessed their work and
they were very successful, bringing a great number to belief.

Throughout Acts, God causes the growth of his church. The role
of the believers was to be faithful, demonstrating the joy of kingdom
life as they taught others of God. It was this evidence of the Holy
Spirit in the lives of believers that brought nonbelievers to repentance
and conversion. What should this tell us about our attempts to expand
God's kingdom?

As news of this successful mission reached Jerusalem, the leaders
felt it was important to make sure the teaching of the gospel was accurate and complete. They sent Barnabas ("son of encouragement") to
Antioch for this reason. When he arrived, he encountered a people
full of God's grace. True to his name, he encouraged them to continue
to grow deeper into the heart of God. He also realized that the rapid
growth of the kingdom would require more teaching than he alone
could do. This led him to Tarsus to find Paul. Barnabas saw this as a
great opportunity to mentor Paul and encourage him in teaching and
preaching. God used Barnabas to call Paul to a ministry that would

change the world. We must never underestimate what God might do through us as we mentor new believers in the faith.

What happens next should stir our hearts deeply. Prophets came from Jerusalem to Antioch and told of distressing times to come. A famine would strike the land. Immediately the believers in Antioch decided to each give whatever they could to help the brothers and sisters living in Judea. People who had once been enemies have now not only become friends, they are caring family. The new believers in Antioch had never seen the faces of their brothers and sisters in Judea. But everything the Christians in Antioch owned was now the possession of their newfound family in Judea. What a beautiful story! What a dramatic change. What clear evidence of the Holy Spirit transforming the hearts of those receiving the word! This is what happens when people truly believe and "turn to the Lord."

How do we respond when we hear of those in need? Are we generous with what we have? Think how generous those first believers were in Jerusalem. Many sold what they had in order to help those in need. Sounds like Jesus, doesn't it? Now the word has spread into new lands. These new believers quickly understand the message. They, too, are willing to give beyond their means. As we pass on the story of the gospel, do we continue to demonstrate that same generous spirit?

"Dear Jesus, may we keep our eyes open to be a mentor to others as you demonstrate your mercy and love in mentoring us. Give me a generous heart toward those in need"

# THE DELIVERANCE OF PETER AND DEATH OF HEROD

## (ACTS 12)

### FIRST DAY READING AND PRAYER

[1] It was about this time that King Herod arrested some who belonged to the church, intending to persecute them. [2] He had James, the brother of John, put to death with the sword. [3] When he saw that this pleased the Jews, he proceeded to seize Peter also. This happened during the Feast of Unleavened Bread. [4] After arresting him, he put him in prison, handing him over to be guarded by four squads of four soldiers each. Herod intended to bring him out for public trial after the Passover. [5] So Peter was kept in prison, but the church was earnestly praying to God for him.

*1. Why do you think Herod arrested those who "belonged to the church?"*

*2. Why do you think Herod took such care with Peter—assigning so many guards to him?*

*3. Can you remember a time in the life of your church when the entire church prayed fervently for someone's well being? What happened?*

## DAY TWO READING AND QUESTIONS

[6] The night before Herod was to bring him to trial, Peter was sleeping between two soldiers, bound with two chains, and sentries stood guard at the entrance. [7] Suddenly an angel of the Lord appeared and a light shone in the cell. He struck Peter on the side and woke him up. "Quick, get up!" he said, and the chains fell off Peter's wrists. [8] Then the angel said to him, "Put on your clothes and sandals." And Peter did so. "Wrap your cloak around you and follow me," the angel told him. [9] Peter followed him out of the prison, but he had no idea that what the angel was doing was really happening; he thought he was seeing a vision. [10] They passed the first and second guards and came to the iron gate leading to the city. It opened for them by itself, and they went through it. When they had walked the length of one street, suddenly the angel left him. [11] Then Peter came to himself and said, "Now I know without a doubt that the Lord sent his angel and rescued me from Herod's clutches and from everything the Jewish people were anticipating."

*1. Why do you think Peter thought he was having a vision?*

*2. What do you think the Jewish people were anticipating?*

*3. Have you ever experienced what you recognized as "divine deliverance?" What happened? How did that event change your life?*

## DAY THREE READING AND QUESTIONS

[12] When this had dawned on him, he went to the house of Mary the mother of John, also called Mark, where many people had gathered and were praying. [13] Peter knocked at the outer entrance, and a servant girl named Rhoda came to answer the door. [14] When she recognized Peter's voice, she was so overjoyed she ran back without opening it and exclaimed, "Peter is at the door!" [15] "You're out of your mind," they told her. When she kept insisting that it was so, they said, "It must be his angel." [16] But Peter kept on knocking, and when they opened the door and saw him, they were astonished. [17] Peter motioned with his hand for them to be quiet and described how the Lord had brought him out of prison. "Tell James and the brothers about this," he said, and then he left for another place. [18] In the morning, there was no small commotion among the soldiers as to what had become of Peter.

*1. Why did Peter go to the house of John's mother, Mary?*

*2. Why didn't the church believe Rhoda?*

*3. When they thought it was Peter's angel, what had they assumed had occurred?*

*4. Reflect on a time when God answered your prayer in a surprising way.*

## DAY FOUR READING AND QUESTIONS

[19] After Herod had a thorough search made for him and did not find him, he cross-examined the guards and ordered that they be executed. Then Herod went from Judea to Caesarea and stayed there a

while. [20] He had been quarreling with the people of Tyre and Sidon; they now joined together and sought an audience with him. Having secured the support of Blastus, a trusted personal servant of the king, they asked for peace, because they depended on the king's country for their food supply. [21] On the appointed day Herod, wearing his royal robes, sat on his throne and delivered a public address to the people. [22] They shouted, "This is the voice of a god, not of a man." [23]

Immediately, because Herod did not give praise to God, an angel of the Lord struck him down, and he was eaten by worms and died. [24] But the word of God continued to increase and spread. [25] When Barnabas and Saul had finished their mission, they returned from Jerusalem, taking with them John, also called Mark.

*1. Why would Herod order the execution of the guards?*

*2. Why do you think Luke informs us of the quarrel Herod had with the people of Tyre and Sidon?*

*3. What do you think is the purpose of the story of the death of Herod?*

## DAY FIVE READING AND QUESTIONS

Reread the entire passage (Acts 12:1-25)

*1. How should we understand this story in the midst of the world's present turmoil?*

*2. Do we earnestly pray for deliverance from evil? Do we expect God to answer?*

*3. What should God's people do in view of the evil so evident in our world?*

# MEDITATION

At times evil in the world seems overwhelming. What are we to do when meaningless violence interrupts our lives? Where is God in such circumstances? Here we have another story that demonstrates to us how God acted and continues to act among his faithful people in the midst of an evil world.

Herod, for no apparent reason, arrested members of the Jerusalem church in order to persecute them. He had James killed. When he saw this pleased those who opposed the church, he had Peter arrested. His intent was surely to kill him as well. He first wanted the entertainment of a public trial— but not until after Passover. Ironic, isn't it? During the festival of celebration for deliverance from Egypt, Herod enslaved Peter. But the God of deliverance was not finished with his miraculous acts of freeing the oppressed.

Apparently, Herod had heard of Peter's previous escape from prison, because he assigned sixteen of his toughest soldiers to guard him. The church was earnestly praying for his deliverance. James had just recently been killed, so it was an especially difficult time. If God were going to deliver, wouldn't he have freed James?

What is hard for us to understand in this story is that God was in no less control when James died just as much as when he freed Peter. Why did he not free James? Who can discern the ways of God? This, however, we know: God was then and is now in control. If our witness is finished and he allows us to come home to him through physical death, who are we to argue against his purposes for our lives?

The response of Peter and the church to his release is both humorous and instructive. Peter had been so affected by James' death that even when the angel freed him he thought he was experiencing a vision. Luke wants us to know Peter expected to die. He was anticipating a torturous trial and a certain death. But suddenly, without explanation, he was miraculously freed by an angel of the Lord. He ran to the house where the church, at that very hour, was meeting to pray for his release. But when he showed up at their door, they could not believe it was him. No one escaped Herod's prisons—unless it was God's will. In spite of the church's lack of faith, God chose to deliver. Peter still had an important role to fill in the proclamation of the kingdom.

The story of Herod's death is an unusual detour for Luke. He leaves the story of the church and informs us of the events that surrounded Herod's demise. Because Herod accepted praise as if he were a god, he was struck down by an angel of the Lord and died a painful death. Luke's message is clear: Herod himself had no power except what God allowed. In the meantime, the word of God continued to increase and spread.

No one or no power can thwart the plans and purposes of God. When appropriate, God will deliver. At other times, God delivers his faithful servants through death itself. It is not ours to question his purposes. It is ours to pray that his will be done and beg for the wisdom to be a part of what he is doing in our world. Make no mistake about it, God is in control.

"Sovereign Lord, teach us to trust your ways."

# PAUL'S JOURNEYS BEGIN
## (ACTS 13:1-13)

## DAY ONE READING AND QUESTIONS

[1] In the church at Antioch there were prophets and teachers: Barnabas, Simeon called Niger, Lucius of Cyrene, Manaen (who had been brought up with Herod the tetrarch) and Saul. [2] While they were worshiping the Lord and fasting, the Holy Spirit said, "Set apart for me Barnabas and Saul for the work to which I have called them." [3] So after they had fasted and prayed, they placed their hands on them and sent them off.

*1. What is the role of the Holy Spirit in these verses?*

*2. Do you fast in connection with worshiping? Why or why not?*

*3. What can we learn from this story on how to send out missionaries?*

## DAY TWO READING AND QUESTIONS

[4] The two of them, sent on their way by the Holy Spirit, went down to Seleucia and sailed from there to Cyprus. [5] When they arrived at Salamis, they proclaimed the word of God in the Jewish synagogues. John was with them as their helper.

*1. What is the role of the Holy Spirit in sending out Saul and Barnabas?*

*2. Why would they proclaim the word of God in the Jewish synagogues?*

*3. Who was John?*

## DAY THREE READING AND QUESTIONS

[6] They traveled through the whole island until they came to Paphos. There they met a Jewish sorcerer and false prophet named Bar-Jesus, [7] who was an attendant of the proconsul, Sergius Paulus. The proconsul, an intelligent man, sent for Barnabas and Saul because he wanted to hear the word of God. [8] But Elymas the sorcerer (for that is what his name means) opposed them and tried to turn the proconsul from the faith.

*1. What is unusual about Bar-Jesus (hint: note his occupation and ethnicity)?*

*2. Why do you think Luke described the proconsul as an intelligent man?*

*3. How do you think Luke would describe "the faith" from which Bar-Jesus tried to turn the proconsul away?*

## DAY FOUR READING AND QUESTIONS

[9] Then Saul, who was also called Paul, filled with the Holy Spirit, looked straight at Elymas and said, [10] "You are a child of the devil and an enemy of everything that is right! You are full of all kinds of deceit

and trickery. Will you never stop perverting the right ways of the Lord? [11] Now the hand of the Lord is against you. You are going to be blind, and for a time you will be unable to see the light of the sun." Immediately mist and darkness came over him, and he groped about, seeking someone to lead him by the hand. [12] When the proconsul saw what had happened, he believed, for he was amazed at the teaching about the Lord. [13] From Paphos, Paul and his companions sailed to Perga in Pamphylia, where John left them to return to Jerusalem.

1. *What explanation does Luke provide for Saul's name change?*

2. *In the teaching about the Lord, what do you think amazed the proconsul?*

3. *Are you amazed by the message and teaching of Jesus? Why or why not?*

## DAY FIVE READING AND QUESTIONS

Reread the entire passage (Acts 13:1-13)

1. *Have you ever spent time with a small group worshiping and fasting? If you have, what did you learn from such experiences?*

2. *Before opposition arises in these stories, what is the general reaction of people who heard the proclamation of the kingdom?*

3. *How can we recover the amazement that the teaching of Jesus brings in these stories?*

# MEDITATION

At the beginning of this reading the leaders of the church in Antioch—prophets and teachers—were worshiping the Lord and fasting. This was apparently a daily practice (revisit Acts 2:42-46). For many believers in today's world, worship is much more familiar than fasting. Fasting is a profitable discipline with great potential to teach. It frees us from the constant whining of our bodily appetites and allows us to focus entirely on the feast of God's presence.

Worship and fasting in the early church was not without a response from God. Luke tells us that during this time of worship and fasting, the Holy Spirit spoke to them. How did the Holy Spirit speak? We do not know. We do know the Holy Spirit made it known that Barnabas and Paul were to set out on a journey. Paul often speaks of God's specific plan for him. He knows God has prepared him as a special vessel to open the kingdom to the Gentiles.

Have you ever wondered what God's mission is for you? Think about this: each of us is unique, with a particular combination of God-given gifts and an original story that is ours alone. To whom are you a special ambassador of the kingdom? I think it would be a beautiful thing to spend time together in worship and fasting, listening for God's voice for his specific purpose of ministry to others in each of our lives. Consider laying hands on each member of your small group, sending each one out into their world of influence with the power of God's Spirit.

Luke's account of Paul's ministry in various places is highly selective. In some locations Luke will tell us much, in others next to nothing. When Paul and Barnabas arrive at Cyprus, Sergius Paulus, the Roman proconsul, wanted to hear their message. He was no common leader simply trying to satisfy his curiosity. He wanted to know of this new teaching. His advisor, a Jewish sorcerer, attempted to turn the proconsul away from their teaching. Paul and Barnabas wasted no words, but boldly challenged their listeners to embrace the faith.

Paul's accusatory question to the sorcerer is interesting: "will you never stop perverting the right ways of the Lord?" God struck the fraudulent sorcerer blind. This is the essence of false teaching—a perversion of the right ways of God leading to blindness. God has a design for our lives. His kingdom is the essence of life. If we do not learn to tune our hearts to God's word, we too are blind.

The proconsul's response? "When he saw what had happened, he believed, for he was amazed at the teaching about the Lord." Paul and Barnabas' teaching had captured the proconsul's heart. Now, through the clear defeat of the false prophet, he willingly embraced "the faith."

"Oh Lord of life and light, may I never be blinded by false teaching. Help me open the eyes of others to the truth of your word."

# PAUL TO PSIDIA

## (13:13-52)

### DAY ONE READING AND QUESTIONS

[13] From Paphos, Paul and his companions sailed to Perga in Pamphylia, where John left them to return to Jerusalem. [14] From Perga they went on to Pisidian Antioch. On the Sabbath they entered the synagogue and sat down. [15] After the reading from the Law and the Prophets, the synagogue rulers sent word to them, saying, "Brothers, if you have a message of encouragement for the people, please speak."

[16] Standing up, Paul motioned with his hand and said: "Men of Israel and you Gentiles who worship God, listen to me! [17] The God of the people of Israel chose our fathers; he made the people prosper during their stay in Egypt, with mighty power he led them out of that country, [18] he endured their conduct for about forty years in the desert, [19] he overthrew seven nations in Canaan and gave their land to his people as their inheritance. [20] All this took about 450 years. "After this, God gave them judges until the time of Samuel the prophet. [21]Then the people asked for a king, and he gave them Saul son of Kish, of the tribe of Benjamin, who ruled forty years. [22] After removing Saul, he made David their king. He testified concerning him: 'I have found David son of Jesse a man after my own heart; he will do everything I want him to do.' [23] "From this man's descendants God has brought to Israel the Savior Jesus, as he promised. [24] Before the coming of Jesus, John preached repentance and baptism to all the people of Israel. [25] As John was completing his work, he said: 'Who do you think I am? I am not that one. No, but he is coming after me, whose sandals I am not worthy to untie.'

1. *Why did Paul begin his defense of belief in Jesus as the Christ with the story of the exodus?*

2. *In his sermon, why did Paul come to Jesus through King David?*

3. *How would you begin a defense of your faith?*

## DAY TWO READING AND QUESTIONS

[26] "Brothers, children of Abraham, and you God-fearing Gentiles, it is to us that this message of salvation has been sent. [27] The people of Jerusalem and their rulers did not recognize Jesus, yet in condemning

him they fulfilled the words of the prophets that are read every Sabbath. [28] Though they found no proper ground for a death sentence, they asked Pilate to have him executed. [29] When they had carried out all that was written about him, they took him down from the tree and laid him in a tomb. [30] But God raised him from the dead, [31] and for many days he was seen by those who had traveled with him from Galilee to Jerusalem. They are now his witnesses to our people. [32] "We tell you the good news: What God promised our fathers [33] he has fulfilled for us, their children, by raising up Jesus. As it is written in the second Psalm: "'You are my Son; today I have become your Father.' [34] The fact that God raised him from the dead, never to decay, is stated in these words: "'I will give you the holy and sure blessings promised to David.' [35] So it is stated elsewhere: "'You will not let your Holy One see decay.' [36] "For when David had served God's purpose in his own generation, he fell asleep; he was buried with his fathers and his body decayed. [37] But the one whom God raised from the dead did not see decay.

1. *What were the Jews unwittingly doing as they illegally tried and executed Jesus?*

2. *What is the "good news" according to this reading?*

3. *Why is this still "good news" for us?*

## DAY THREE READING AND QUESTIONS

[38] "Therefore, my brothers, I want you to know that through Jesus the forgiveness of sins is proclaimed to you. [39] Through him everyone who believes is justified from everything you could not be justified from by the law of Moses. [40] Take care that what the prophets have said does not happen to you: [41] "'Look, you scoffers, wonder and perish, for I am

going to do something in your days that you would never believe, even if someone told you.'" [42] As Paul and Barnabas were leaving the synagogue, the people invited them to speak further about these things on the next Sabbath. [43] When the congregation was dismissed, many of the Jews and devout converts to Judaism followed Paul and Barnabas, who talked with them and urged them to continue in the grace of God.

*1. What does it mean to "believe in Jesus"? Do you believe?*

*2. What could one "not be justified from" by the Law of Moses?*

*3. Why were Paul and Barnabas invited back the next Sabbath?*

## DAY FOUR READING AND QUESTIONS

[44] On the next Sabbath almost the whole city gathered to hear the word of the Lord. [45] When the Jews saw the crowds, they were filled with jealousy and talked abusively against what Paul was saying. [46]Then Paul and Barnabas answered them boldly: "We had to speak the word of God to you first. Since you reject it and do not consider yourselves worthy of eternal life, we now turn to the Gentiles. [47] For this is what the Lord has commanded us: "'I have made you a light for the Gentiles, that you may bring salvation to the ends of the earth.'" [48]When the Gentiles heard this, they were glad and honored the word of the Lord; and all who were appointed for eternal life believed. [49]The word of the Lord spread through the whole region. [50] But the Jews incited the God-fearing women of high standing and the leading men of the city. They stirred up persecution against Paul and Barnabas, and expelled them from their region. [51] So they shook the dust from their feet in protest against them and went to Iconium. [52] And the disciples were filled with joy and with the Holy Spirit.

1. What is the evidence of Paul's successful communication of the good news?

2. What caused the Jewish leaders to turn away from Paul and Barnabas?

3. How do you think the Gentiles "honored the word of the Lord?" Do we so honor it?

## DAY FIVE READING AND QUESTIONS

Reread the entire passage (Acts 13:13-52)

1. What connection does the deliverance of the children of Israel from Egypt have with the story of Jesus?

2. What is emphasized in the life of Jesus in this sermon?

3. Why did the Jews refuse to hear, while many of the Gentiles heard and believed?

4. What, in our culture, keeps us from hearing the offer of "eternal life" from God?

# MEDITATION

When it came to proving the truth of his message to Jews, Paul did not resort to miracles but to reminding them of their history. He retells the story of God's faithfulness with Israel. In much the same way that Peter told the story at Pentecost, Paul continues to tell the story. It begins with a delivering God and ends with a delivering God. It began as Israel's story of deliverance. It was Jesus' message of salvation. It was Peter's proclamation of deliverance. It was the focus of Paul's preaching. It should be the central story of our lives in God's kingdom. Is it our story?

Paul begins his message of encouragement with a quick summary of God's deliverance of Israel. He then recalls the story of David, which gives Paul a bridge to Jesus, the promised Savior. He explains that John the Baptist prepared for Jesus' message by calling people to repentance and baptism. The Jewish leaders did not recognize Jesus and unknowingly fulfilled all the prophecies concerning the suffering and death of the Messiah. This allows Paul to arrive at the central part of his message—the good news. God has fulfilled the promises given long ago through the raising of Jesus from the dead. Quoting various Old Testament prophecies, Paul makes it clear that Jesus is indeed the fulfillment of God's purposes. Forgiveness of sins is now available. What the Law could not do, Jesus has done for those who believe in him.

Those listening received the message with joy. As Paul concluded, the people wanted more. The following Sabbath the entire city gathered. Luke makes it clear throughout Acts that whenever the message was preached to those who were open to hear the word, it was received with joy and many obeyed the gospel. But there are also those who refuse to hear. Jealousy, self-interest, an unwillingness to repent caused some to turn away and even to try to keep Paul from preaching. The acceptance and refusal of the gospel continues to this day.

So what will we do with the message of Jesus? Will we believe and accept the life offered in his name? Might it be that we have accepted our culture's view of life as superior to life in Jesus? Might it be that we have refused "eternal life" and turned away from authentic discipleship in order to remain secure in our secular comforts? Luke does not tell these stories out of historical interest—he sees them as living stories that allow us to discern the truth of the kingdom of God. Have we embraced the ancient promises of God, fulfilled in the life and ministry, death and resurrection of Jesus? Do we believe?

"Lord of deliverance, free us from the bondage of our secular desires so that we might hear and accept your offer for life in Jesus."

# THE JOURNEY CONTINUES

### (ACTS 14:1-28)

## DAY ONE READING AND QUESTIONS

[1] At Iconium Paul and Barnabas went as usual into the Jewish synagogue. There they spoke so effectively that a great number of Jews and Gentiles believed. [2] But the Jews who refused to believe stirred up the Gentiles and poisoned their minds against the brothers. [3] So Paul and Barnabas spent considerable time there, speaking boldly for the Lord, who confirmed the message of his grace by enabling them to do miraculous signs and wonders. [4] The people of the city were divided; some sided with the Jews, others with the apostles. [5] There was a plot afoot among the Gentiles and Jews, together with their leaders, to mistreat them and stone them. [6] But they found out about it and fled to the Lycaonian cities of Lystra and Derbe and to the surrounding country, [7] where they continued to preach the good news.

*1. What, once again, is the initial effect of preaching the gospel?*

*2. Who confirmed the message? How?*

*3. What can we learn from Paul and Barnabas as they constantly dealt with opposition?*

## DAY TWO READING AND QUESTIONS

[8] In Lystra there sat a man crippled in his feet, who was lame from birth and had never walked. [9] He listened to Paul as he was speaking. Paul looked directly at him, saw that he had faith to be healed [10] and called out, "Stand up on your feet!" At that, the man jumped up and began to walk. [11] When the crowd saw what Paul had done, they shouted in the Lycaonian language, "The gods have come down to us in human form!" [12] Barnabas they called Zeus, and Paul they called Hermes because he was the chief speaker. [13] The priest of Zeus, whose temple was just outside the city, brought bulls and wreaths to the city gates because he and the crowd wanted to offer sacrifices to them.

*1. How quickly was the man, lame from birth, healed completely? Why is this significant?*

*2. Why did the people associate Paul and Barnabas with pagan gods?*

*3. How would you have responded had you been in Paul and Barnabas' situation?*

## DAY THREE READING AND QUESTIONS

[14] But when the apostles Barnabas and Paul heard of this, they tore their clothes and rushed out into the crowd, shouting: [15] "Men, why are you doing this? We too are only men, human like you. We are bringing you good news, telling you to turn from these worthless

things to the living God, who made heaven and earth and sea and everything in them. [16] In the past, he let all nations go their own way. [17] Yet he has not left himself without testimony: He has shown kindness by giving you rain from heaven and crops in their seasons; he provides you with plenty of food and fills your hearts with joy." [18] Even with these words, they had difficulty keeping the crowd from sacrificing to them. [19] Then some Jews came from Antioch and Iconium and won the crowd over. They stoned Paul and dragged him outside the city, thinking he was dead. [20] But after the disciples had gathered around him, he got up and went back into the city. The next day he and Barnabas left for Derbe.

1. *Why were Barnabas and Paul so upset with the crowds' misunderstanding?*

2. *What was the good news preached in this city?*

3. *Why did the crowd turn from worshipers into a violent mob in such a short time?*

## DAY FOUR READING AND QUESTIONS

[21] They preached the good news in that city and won a large number of disciples. Then they returned to Lystra, Iconium and Antioch, [22]strengthening the disciples and encouraging them to remain true to the faith. "We must go through many hardships to enter the kingdom of God," they said. [23] Paul and Barnabas appointed elders for them in each church and, with prayer and fasting, committed them to the Lord, in whom they had put their trust. [24] After going through Pisidia, they came into Pamphylia, [25] and when they had preached the word in Perga, they went down to Attalia. [26] From Attalia they sailed back to

Antioch, where they had been committed to the grace of God for the work they had now completed. [27] On arriving there, they gathered the church together and reported all that God had done through them and how he had opened the door of faith to the Gentiles. [28] And they stayed there a long time with the disciples.

1. *What effect did Paul's stoning have on his willingness to preach the gospel?*

2. *Why do you think Paul and Barnabas were so determined to preach the good news, no matter what the results?*

3. *What did Paul and Barnabas do as they returned to the cities where they had previously preached? Do you find this surprising? If so, why?*

## DAY FIVE READING AND QUESTIONS

Reread the entire passage (Acts 14:1-28)

1. *Have you ever experienced someone intentionally trying to interfere with work you were doing for the Lord? How did you respond?*

2. *Why was it important that the crippled man had the "faith to be healed"?*

3. *Do we have the faith to allow God to do his marvelous work through us?*

## MEDITATION

When Paul and Barnabas left Iconium to escape harm, they headed to Lystra and Derbe, which were small cities off the main trade routes. There were no Jewish synagogues in these small pagan towns. Did this deter Paul and Barnabas? Not at all. As they spoke of Jesus and the new life he offers, they found believers. In Lystra the message visibly moved a man lame from birth. What a wonderful opportunity to show the power of new life in Jesus! Once again we see the incredible power of authentic healing. A man who had never walked jumped to his feet and walked as if he had done it all his life.

Those witnessing this wonderful miracle didn't know what to think. They had never seen such a thing. The people mistakenly assumed Paul and Barnabas were gods. Paul would have none of this! He would not allow the power of the true God to be attributed to pagan gods. As he pleads with them to hear his message of the true God, distracters quickly turned the crowd from worship to disdain. They drew Paul out of the city and stoned him, assuming they had killed him. Luke's account here is surely understated. Stoning was no small thing. Large rocks crushed the accused. This was no pebble-throwing incident. Paul was bloody, broken, and unconscious. Yet the text simply notes that when believers surrounded him, he got up and walked back to the city. Not only that, but after leaving and preaching in other cities, he returned to Lystra to encourage the believers there. The clear message here is the unstoppable nature of the good news of life in Jesus. Paul is not intended to be the hero of this story. He is simply the one given the grace to proclaim the eternal truth of God's kingdom. And God would sustain him until his work was completed.

In Paul and Barnabas' return to the churches they had started, we see one of the most important teachings in Acts. Christian leaders were constantly involved in prayer, fasting, and worship. It led to great confidence in the active power and guidance of God. This allowed them to entrust new converts with the responsibility to lead as servants. They were not alone in their roles of leadership. Paul and Barnabas believed in the active role of the Holy Spirit in the lives of these leaders. What was there to fear?

This segment of the message ends with the victorious return of the missionaries to their sending church. They had successfully accomplished their mission and returned with wonderful stories of God's activity in foreign lands.

What do we know of the early church up to this point? We know it was growing rapidly because of God's blessings. We know the church had a deep sense of its mission— they knew God had a purpose for them, and it was to proclaim the word of God to others. The picture of church in Acts is a community spending much time in worship, prayer, and fasting. If there is a pattern of the church that Luke wants us to see, this is it.

"Father, thank you for the privilege of sharing the good news of life in Jesus. May we have the confidence and courage of Paul and Barnabas to proclaim your word without fear."

# THE JERUSALEM COUNCIL
## (ACTS 15:1-21)

### DAY ONE READING AND QUESTIONS

[1] Some men came down from Judea to Antioch and were teaching the brothers: "Unless you are circumcised, according to the custom taught by Moses, you cannot be saved." [2] This brought Paul and Barnabas into sharp dispute and debate with them. So Paul and Barnabas were appointed, along with some other believers, to go up to Jerusalem to see the apostles and elders about this question. [3] The church sent them on their way, and as they traveled through Phoenicia and Samaria, they told how the Gentiles had been converted. This news made all the brothers very glad.

*1. Why do you think circumcision was such an important issue for those who came from Judea?*

*2. What can we learn from the church in Antioch about dealing with disputes?*

*3. Why do you think those in Samaria and Phoenicia accepted the news of the spread of the gospel with gladness?*

## DAY TWO READING AND QUESTIONS

⁴ When they came to Jerusalem, they were welcomed by the church and the apostles and elders, to whom they reported everything God had done through them. ⁵ Then some of the believers who belonged to the party of the Pharisees stood up and said, "The Gentiles must be circumcised and required to obey the law of Moses."

*1. How were Paul and Barnabas received by the Jerusalem church?*

*2. What provoked the statement by the Pharisees?*

*3. Can you think of similar doctrinal disputes in churches today? How should we attempt to resolve these issues?*

## DAY THREE READING AND QUESTIONS

⁶ The apostles and elders met to consider this question. ⁷ After much discussion, Peter got up and addressed them: "Brothers, you know that some time ago God made a choice among you that the Gentiles might hear from my lips the message of the gospel and believe. ⁸ God, who knows the heart, showed that he accepted them by giving the Holy Spirit to them, just as he did to us. ⁹ He made no distinction between us and them, for he purified their hearts by faith. ¹⁰ Now then, why do you try to test God by putting on the necks of the disciples a yoke that neither we nor our fathers have been able to bear? ¹¹ No! We believe it is through the grace of our Lord Jesus that we are saved, just as they are."

*1. Why do you think Peter was the one to first address the assembly after "much discussion"?*

*2. To what event does Peter refer in explaining what he thought was a proper solution?*

*3. What was the basis of salvation according to Peter? Why is this applicable to the question of whether circumcision was necessary?*

## DAY FOUR READING AND QUESTIONS

[12] The whole assembly became silent as they listened to Barnabas and Paul telling about the miraculous signs and wonders God had done among the Gentiles through them. [13] When they finished, James spoke up: "Brothers, listen to me. [14] Simon has described to us how God at first showed his concern by taking from the Gentiles a people for himself. [15] The words of the prophets are in agreement with this, as it is written: [16] "'After this I will return and rebuild David's fallen tent. Its ruins I will rebuild, and I will restore it, [17] that the remnant of men may seek the Lord, and all the Gentiles who bear my name, says the Lord, who does these things' [18] that have been known for ages. [19] "It is my judgment, therefore, that we should not make it difficult for the Gentiles who are turning to God. [20] Instead we should write to them, telling them to abstain from food polluted by idols, from sexual immorality, from the meat of strangled animals and from blood. [21] For Moses has been preached in every city from the earliest times and is read in the synagogues on every Sabbath."

*1. What was different about what Paul and Barnabas described in these verses and what they had reported in verse 4?*

*2. To what does James refer which builds on Peter's experience with the Gentiles?*

*3. Why do you think James ties certain prohibitions to the fact that Moses was preached in every city?*

## DAY FIVE READING AND QUESTIONS

Reread the entire passage (Acts 15:1-21)

*1. Why do you think the Pharisees in the church of Jerusalem were so concerned about obedience to the Law of Moses?*

*2. Are there areas of our belief systems that might be analogous to those of the Pharisees? If so, what can we learn from this story to assist us in finding godly solutions to our disagreements over such issues?*

*3. What does James reference to Old Testament prophecies, which were dismissed or misunderstood, tell us about the way we read Scripture?*

## MEDITATION

The great divide of biblical times was the social and religious barrier between Jews and the rest of the world—one that would not be easily broken.

We should not dismiss as evil or even legalistic those who continued to believe in the necessity of circumcision. They were fully convinced that the Law of Moses was a necessary step to Jesus. They were so fervent in their belief that they traveled to Antioch to teach that circumcision was still essential. Paul and Barnabas had just returned from an incredible journey where they had witnessed God's working among the Gentiles in amazing ways. They knew God had placed no requirement of circumcision on the Gentile converts.

128

However, they were not able to settle the dispute without help.

This issue threatened to divide the church. It was a profound problem. Its solution stands as an important model of conflict resolution. Those concerned traveled to Jerusalem to seek the help of the leaders there. Peter told the story of Cornelius' conversion one more time. God's giving the Gentiles the Holy Spirit before baptism was an undeniable demonstration of his favor towards them, making clear that he made no distinction between the circumcised and the uncircumcised when it came to giving the Spirit.

We must not miss Peter's point about imposing on the Gentiles a yoke the Jews themselves could not bear. What they were insisting others do was something they themselves could not do! No one could be justified through obedience to God's law. That was the essence of the good news of Jesus—we are justified by God's grace. By their insistence on following the Law, they were, in essence, canceling out the good news. Have we done similar things with our own belief systems?

Now Paul and Barnabas retell their experiences in pagan lands. This time they focus on the signs and wonders God had done. This was indisputable evidence that God had chosen to receive the Gentiles by faith—the same basis on which the Jews were received.

James then stands up and quotes a passage from Amos 9 to demonstrate that God has always desired to save the Gentiles. God's plan was to bring from the ruins of David's nation a kingdom that would be for all believers, regardless of their ethnicity. God had always loved the Gentiles. How could the Pharisees—known for their thorough knowledge of Scripture—have missed this?

May we learn from this great event in church history to seek godly wisdom from wise believers. May we keep our hearts open to know God's will more deeply as we confront the questions raised in our ever-changing culture.

"Loving God, help us see all peoples of the world as you see them. May we never impede their journey toward you."

# A LETTER TO GENTILE BELIEVERS

## (ACTS 15:22-35)

### DAY ONE READING AND QUESTIONS

[22] Then the apostles and elders, with the whole church, decided to choose some of their own men and send them to Antioch with Paul and Barnabas. They chose Judas (called Barsabbas) and Silas, two men who were leaders among the brothers.

> *1. Why do you think the church decided to send some of their own men with Paul and Barnabas?*

> *2. Why do you think Luke chose to give us the men's names?*

> *3. What can we learn from this response to the circumcision question?*

### DAY TWO READING AND QUESTIONS

[23] With them they sent the following letter: The apostles and elders, your brothers, To the Gentile believers in Antioch, Syria and Cilicia: Greetings. [24] We have heard that some went out from us without our

authorization and disturbed you, troubling your minds by what they said. [25] So we all agreed to choose some men and send them to you with our dear friends Barnabas and Paul— 26 men who have risked their lives for the name of our Lord Jesus Christ. [27] Therefore we are sending Judas and Silas to confirm by word of mouth what we are writing.

1. *Since they were sending a group to communicate their concerns, why do you think the apostles and elders sent a letter as well?*

2. *Why was it significant that those who had originally gone out and created the problem were not "authorized" representatives?*

3. *Why did the Jerusalem leaders send men along with the letter? What was their role?*

## DAY THREE READING AND QUESTIONS

[28] It seemed good to the Holy Spirit and to us not to burden you with anything beyond the following requirements: [29] You are to abstain from food sacrificed to idols, from blood, from the meat of strangled animals and from sexual immorality. You will do well to avoid these things. Farewell.

1. *What did the church leaders understand as the role of the Holy Spirit in this whole process?*

2. *Why did those in Jerusalem list certain activities from which the Gentiles were to abstain?*

3. *Are you surprised by the brevity of the letter? Why or why not?*

## DAY FOUR READING AND QUESTIONS

[30] The men were sent off and went down to Antioch, where they gathered the church together and delivered the letter. [31] The people read it and were glad for its encouraging message. [32] Judas and Silas, who themselves were prophets, said much to encourage and strengthen the brothers. [33] After spending some time there, they were sent off by the brothers with the blessing of peace to return to those who had sent them. [34] But Paul and Barnabas remained in Antioch, where they and many others taught and preached the word of the Lord.

1. *Why do you think the message was encouraging?*

2. *How did Judas and Silas play an important role in helping strengthen the church?*

3. *What was the result of this major conflict in the preaching of the word of the Lord?*

## DAY FIVE READING AND QUESTIONS

Reread the entire passage (Acts 15:22-35)

1. *What do you think might have happened if the leaders in the church in Jerusalem had decided that, for the sake of peace, the Gentiles should follow the Law of Moses?*

2. *Does this entire episode (from the trouble in Antioch to the return of Paul and Barnabas) encourage or discourage you? Why?*

*3. What do you think is the most important lesson we can learn from this event?*

# MEDITATION

For the sake of the advancement of truth, the Gentiles were to abstain from meat sacrificed to idols, from sexual immorality, and from meat that had not been properly drained of blood. The entire assembly concluded these teachings were valid. Luke informs us that the Holy Spirit was fully involved in this decision. This decision was included in the letter to the Gentile believers as a way of helping them enter into fellowship with their Jewish brethren. The list of prohibited activities all had to do with the Gentiles' previous worship rituals. As difficult as it was for the Jews to give up their view of circumcision, the Gentiles must also give up things that for them were sacred—and equally challenging to remove from their thinking. This is difficult for us to imagine. But if you had been raised to eat meat offered to the gods, to see certain sexual behavior (temple prostitution) as necessary to gain the gods' favor, if you had been taught to drink blood as a sign of faithfulness—it would not be easy to turn from such practices. However, this is exactly what the Holy Spirit called them to do.

This allows Paul later to explain that eating meat sacrificed to idols was not wrong in and of itself. It depended on how one understood the eating of such meat. Clearly, sexual immorality is never right. It was included in James' list because of its connection to pagan worship practices.

This whole episode serves as a wonderful example of how to resolve conflict. Identify the problem, call the disputing parties together, spend much time in prayer and study—and allow the Holy Spirit to work in all hearts to bring a God-honoring resolution. In this way, we allow Jesus to continue to work in his church.

Too often we are more concerned about our rights and our own personal desires that at times cause divisions in our churches. May we be in constant prayer that God would break our selfish hearts and give us the wisdom to know when it is proper to concede our own desires for the sake of peace in the church.

"Prince of Peace, give us the wisdom to resolve our disputes through submission to your will and out of a deep love for our brothers and sisters."

# DISAGREEMENT AND A NEW JOURNEY
## (ACTS 15:36-16:15)

### DAY ONE READING AND QUESTIONS

[36] Some time later Paul said to Barnabas, "Let us go back and visit the brothers in all the towns where we preached the word of the Lord and see how they are doing." [37] Barnabas wanted to take John, also called Mark, with them, [38] but Paul did not think it wise to take him, because he had deserted them in Pamphylia and had not continued with them in the work. [39] They had such a sharp disagreement that they parted company. Barnabas took Mark and sailed for Cyprus, [40] but Paul chose Silas and left, commended by the brothers to the grace of the Lord. [41] He went through Syria and Cilicia, strengthening the churches.

*1. Why do you think Paul and Barnabas disagreed on the matter of John Mark?*

*2. Why is the commendation of the brothers toward Paul significant?*

*3. Is this parting of the ways between Paul and Barnabas a negative or positive episode in the work they would do for the church?*

## DAY TWO READING AND QUESTIONS

[1] He came to Derbe and then to Lystra, where a disciple named Timothy lived, whose mother was a Jewess and a believer, but whose father was a Greek. [2] The brothers at Lystra and Iconium spoke well of him. [3] Paul wanted to take him along on the journey, so he circumcised him because of the Jews who lived in that area, for they all knew that his father was a Greek. [4] As they traveled from town to town, they delivered the decisions reached by the apostles and elders in Jerusalem for the people to obey. [5] So the churches were strengthened in the faith and grew daily in numbers.

*1. What happened the last time Paul was in Derbe and Lystra?*

*2. Why did Paul have Timothy circumcised when the elders and apostles in Jerusalem just deemed it unnecessary?*

*3. What are the implications for us of Paul's decision to circumcise Timothy as we confront contemporary issues that might be divisive?*

## DAY THREE READING AND QUESTIONS

[6] Paul and his companions traveled throughout the region of Phrygia and Galatia, having been kept by the Holy Spirit from preaching the word in the province of Asia. [7] When they came to the

border of Mysia, they tried to enter Bithynia, but the Spirit of Jesus would not allow them to. [8] So they passed by Mysia and went down to Troas. [9]During the night Paul had a vision of a man of Macedonia standing and begging him, "Come over to Macedonia and help us." [10] After Paul had seen the vision, we got ready at once to leave for Macedonia, concluding that God had called us to preach the gospel to them.

1. *What do you think is the difference between Luke's use of "Holy Spirit" and the "Spirit of Jesus"?*

2. *Why do you think Paul was prohibited from going certain places?*

3. *How might the Holy Spirit prohibit us today from certain activities? Have you ever experienced a strong leading of the Spirit?*

## DAY FOUR READING AND QUESTIONS

[11] From Troas we put out to sea and sailed straight for Samothrace, and the next day on to Neapolis. [12] From there we traveled to Philippi, a Roman colony and the leading city of that district of Macedonia. And we stayed there several days. [13] On the Sabbath we went outside the city gate to the river, where we expected to find a place of prayer. We sat down and began to speak to the women who had gathered there. [14] One of those listening was a woman named Lydia, a dealer in purple cloth from the city of Thyatira, who was a worshiper of God. The Lord opened her heart to respond to Paul's message. [15] When she and the members of her household were baptized, she invited us to her home. "If you consider me a believer in the Lord," she said, "come and stay at my house." And she persuaded us.

*1. Note that the pronouns change from third person to first person at Troas. What does that likely indicate about the writer's participation in the story?*

*2. Why do you think Paul and his group went to the river to find a place of prayer on the Sabbath?*

*3. Do you remember when your heart was opened to hear the message of truth? Take a moment and savor that memory.*

## DAY FIVE READING AND QUESTIONS

Reread the entire passage (Acts 15:36-16:15)

*1. Are you surprised that Paul returned so quickly to Derbe and Lystra? Why or why not?*

*2. What was the result of reading the decision of the apostles and elders to the churches Paul visited?*

*3. How directly do you think God is guiding us in our lives today?*

## MEDITATION

Paul apparently could not stay still for long. He wanted to see how the churches he and Barnabas had planted were doing. It is here that Luke tells us of a disagreement between Paul and Barnabas that ultimately causes them to part ways. I think Luke includes this incident because it shows us that not all division is counterproductive for the kingdom. Barnabas was able to mentor John Mark, and with Paul going in another direction with Silas, twice as many young churches received attention.

Paul's courage is amazing. He did not hesitate to return to an area where he was stoned and left for dead. While strengthening the churches in Lystra and Iconium, Paul came to know a young man named Timothy. He is the one to whom Paul would ultimately entrust his evangelistic mantle after his death (read 2 Timothy). He was Paul's "son in the faith." Paul's model of mentoring Timothy merits our attention. Paul understood the potential of Timothy's contribution to building churches—that is why he chose to have him circumcised. Because his father was Greek, Timothy had not been circumcised as an infant. It is ironic that the message Paul (along with Timothy) would continue to take to the churches was that circumcision was not necessary for the Gentile believer. Yet Paul would allow nothing to hinder the spread of the good news among the Jews and thus had Timothy circumcised. It was not necessary, but for the good of the propagation of the gospel, it was the right thing to do.

Prohibited by the Holy Spirit to preach in Asia, Paul experienced "the Macedonian call." The first city he entered in that province was Philippi. There was no synagogue in the city, so Paul went to the river outside the town on the Sabbath, knowing he would find a small gathering of Jews there for prayer. Here he encountered Lydia and a group of women who had gathered for prayer. It is significant that Paul preached to them. He did not distinguish between men and women regarding their value in the kingdom. Lydia is clearly the focus of this story. All the good that happened in Philippi (see Paul's letter to the Philippians) began with a leading merchant woman in that city. It is likely that the church continued to meet in her house as it grew.

Note that Luke tells us it was God who opened Lydia's heart. It is God's work to open the hearts and minds of those without Jesus. Where did we ever get the idea that preaching the gospel and getting people to respond is up to us? Wherever we go, if we go in the name of Jesus, God will do his work. In my experience in teaching and preaching, God never fails to show up—even when I mess up. Take courage, God does not depend on our expertise to change people's hearts. He calls only for our faithfulness in proclaiming his truth.

"Savior of the world, open my eyes to those seeking the truth. Help me be faithful in proclaiming the good news of Jesus to all I encounter, knowing you are at work through me."

# A JAILOR CONVERTED
## (ACTS 16:16-40)

### DAY ONE READING AND QUESTIONS

[16] Once when we were going to the place of prayer, we were met by a slave girl who had a spirit by which she predicted the future. She earned a great deal of money for her owners by fortune-telling. [17] This girl followed Paul and the rest of us, shouting, "These men are servants of the Most High God, who are telling you the way to be saved." [18] She kept this up for many days. Finally Paul became so troubled that he turned around and said to the spirit, "In the name of Jesus Christ I command you to come out of her!" At that moment the spirit left her.

*1. What does this passage indicate in terms of how often Paul and his company went to the river to pray?*

*2. Why do you think the proclamation of the slave girl troubled Paul?*

*3. How often do you take time to pray? Do you have or have you ever considered having a place of prayer?*

## DAY TWO READING AND QUESTIONS

[19] When the owners of the slave girl realized that their hope of making money was gone, they seized Paul and Silas and dragged them into the marketplace to face the authorities. [20] They brought them before the magistrates and said, "These men are Jews, and are throwing our city into an uproar [21] by advocating customs unlawful for us Romans to accept or practice." [22] The crowd joined in the attack against Paul and Silas, and the magistrates ordered them to be stripped and beaten. [23] After they had been severely flogged, they were thrown into prison, and the jailer was commanded to guard them carefully. [24]Upon receiving such orders, he put them in the inner cell and fastened their feet in the stocks.

*1. What was the motivation for Paul and Silas being placed under "citizen's arrest"?*

*2. What was the official charge placed against them?*

*3. Why was the crowd so seemingly fickle and willing to join in the accusations against Paul and Silas?*

## DAY THREE READING AND QUESTIONS

[25] About midnight Paul and Silas were praying and singing hymns to God, and the other prisoners were listening to them. [26] Suddenly there was such a violent earthquake that the foundations of the prison

were shaken. At once all the prison doors flew open, and everybody's chains came loose. [27] The jailer woke up, and when he saw the prison doors open, he drew his sword and was about to kill himself because he thought the prisoners had escaped. [28] But Paul shouted, "Don't harm yourself! We are all here!" [29] The jailer called for lights, rushed in and fell trembling before Paul and Silas. [30] He then brought them out and asked, "Sirs, what must I do to be saved?" [31] They replied, "Believe in the Lord Jesus, and you will be saved—you and your household." [32]Then they spoke the word of the Lord to him and to all the others in his house. [33] At that hour of the night the jailer took them and washed their wounds; then immediately he and all his family were baptized. [34] The jailer brought them into his house and set a meal before them; he was filled with joy because he had come to believe in God—he and his whole family.

1. *By the prisoners response to Paul and Silas' singing, what can we learn of early Christian singing?*

2. *Why would the jailer ask Paul what he had to do to be saved? What was Paul's response?*

3. *What filled the jailor and his house with joy? Do we express that joy?*

## DAY FOUR READING AND QUESTIONS

[35] When it was daylight, the magistrates sent their officers to the jailer with the order: "Release those men." [36] The jailer told Paul, "The magistrates have ordered that you and Silas be released. Now you can leave. Go in peace." [37] But Paul said to the officers: "They beat us publicly without a trial, even though we are Roman citizens, and

threw us into prison. And now do they want to get rid of us quietly? No! Let them come themselves and escort us out." [38] The officers reported this to the magistrates, and when they heard that Paul and Silas were Roman citizens, they were alarmed. [39] They came to appease them and escorted them from the prison, requesting them to leave the city. [40] After Paul and Silas came out of the prison, they went to Lydia's house, where they met with the brothers and encouraged them. Then they left.

*1. Why do you think the magistrates wanted Paul and Silas released?*

*2. Why wouldn't Paul just leave? Was he right to be so insistent?*

*3. Are there times when we, like Paul, should stand for our rights? When should we do this, and when should we simply do what is asked of us?*

## DAY FIVE READING AND QUESTIONS

Reread the entire passage (Acts 16:16-40)

*1. What surprises you most about this story?*

*2. Suggestion: Read the letter to the Philippians to refresh you memory of what developed in that church.*

*3. While we may not be able to sing and pray at our workplace, what are ways that we can demonstrate the joy we have because of our belief in God through Jesus Christ?*

# MEDITATION

In this episode, as Paul and his company went to the place of prayer, a possessed slave girl followed them saying, "Listen to these men from the true God, they will tell you how to be saved." After a period of time, Paul cast out the spirit in the name of Jesus. Tragically, from her owners' point of view her only value was the ability to make them money. Her owners wanted Paul and Silas punished for their loss. They incited the crowd to join them in accusing Paul and Silas of insurrection. Brought before uninterested magistrates, their accusations were accepted without any form of questioning. They ordered Paul and Silas to be beaten and thrown into the maximum-security area of the local jail.

How did Paul and Silas react to all this mistreatment? Were they bitter towards God? Did they call on God to destroy the heathens who falsely accused them? No, they sang songs of praise to God and lifted his name in prayer. Is a flogging and imprisonment a time for praise and thanksgiving? For Paul and Silas, the surprising answer is "yes." We know their behavior deeply influenced the prisoners because after the earthquake, instead of fleeing, they all stayed within the confines of the shattered walls. The jailor was going to take his own life until he heard Paul's voice assure him the prisoners were all still there. The jailor, too, must have been listening to their songs and prayers. He wanted the life Paul and Silas had. He joyfully washed their wounds, and they preached the good news of God's kingdom. The jailor and his household were baptized into God's salvation life. The summary statement of the jailor's conversion is instructive. He and his household were filled with joy because they believed in God. Is there any other response that makes sense? When one truly believes the message of Jesus, of living in the kingdom of God and walking with the Holy Spirit, how can one not be filled with joy?

The end of this episode is interesting. The magistrates now knew of their terrible mistake. Paul was a Roman citizen. They had beaten and imprisoned a Roman citizen. So they sent the message to have Paul and Silas released. Why did Paul refuse to do so? It seems inconsistent that Paul was so forgiving in some cases, but here insists the magistrates own up to their wrongful behavior. We need to be very careful not to use this incident in Paul's life in defense of us insisting on our rights. Paul was not interested in preserving his rights. Rather, he used this event as an opportunity to secure the unimpeded growth of the church in that city. His apparent "belligerent behavior" was not about his mistreatment—his passion to expand the kingdom is what motivated this behavior. If we want to imitate Paul, it begins with a selfless passion for God's kingdom and full submission to Jesus Christ as Lord.

"Lord, fill me with the wisdom so that, in every situation, I might do what best advances your kingdom."

# PAUL IN THESSALONICA AND BEREA
## (ACTS 17:1-15)

### DAY ONE READING AND QUESTIONS

[1] When they had passed through Amphipolis and Apollonia, they came to Thessalonica, where there was a Jewish synagogue. [2] As his custom was, Paul went into the synagogue, and on three Sabbath days he reasoned with them from the Scriptures, [3] explaining and proving

that the Christ had to suffer and rise from the dead. "This Jesus I am proclaiming to you is the Christ," he said. ⁴ Some of the Jews were persuaded and joined Paul and Silas, as did a large number of God-fearing Greeks and not a few prominent women.

*1. What verbs did Luke use to describe Paul's actions in Thessalonica?*

*2. What was the response to the message?*

*3. What can we learn from Paul's approach to teaching in the synagogues?*

## DAY TWO READING AND QUESTIONS

⁵ But the Jews were jealous; so they rounded up some bad characters from the marketplace, formed a mob and started a riot in the city. They rushed to Jason's house in search of Paul and Silas in order to bring them out to the crowd. ⁶ But when they did not find them, they dragged Jason and some other brothers before the city officials, shouting: "These men who have caused trouble all over the world have now come here, ⁷ and Jason has welcomed them into his house. They are all defying Caesar's decrees, saying that there is another king, one called Jesus." ⁸ When they heard this, the crowd and the city officials were thrown into turmoil. ⁹ Then they made Jason and the others post bond and let them go.

*1. What motivated those who took action against Paul and Silas?*

*2. Of what are Paul and Silas accused?*

*3. By now we see a clear pattern of resistance against the gospel. What should this tell us about our attempts to teach nonbelievers about Jesus?*

## DAY THREE READING AND QUESTIONS

[10] As soon as it was night, the brothers sent Paul and Silas away to Berea. On arriving there, they went to the Jewish synagogue. [11] Now the Bereans were of more noble character than the Thessalonians, for they received the message with great eagerness and examined the Scriptures every day to see if what Paul said was true. [12] Many of the Jews believed, as did also a number of prominent Greek women and many Greek men.

1. *Why is it surprising that as soon as Paul and Silas "escaped" Thessalonica and arrived in Berea, they immediately went to the synagogue? What does this tell us about their faith?*

2. *Why were the Bereans "more noble"?*

3. *What was the result of Paul's teaching in Berea? What should this tell us about our preaching and teaching?*

## DAY FOUR READING AND QUESTIONS

[13] When the Jews in Thessalonica learned that Paul was preaching the word of God at Berea, they went there too, agitating the crowds and stirring them up. [14] The brothers immediately sent Paul to the coast, but Silas and Timothy stayed at Berea. [15] The men who escorted Paul brought him to Athens and then left with instructions for Silas and Timothy to join him as soon as possible.

1. *Why do you think those opposed to Paul and his teaching were so relentless in hunting him down?*

2. *In all the opposition to the gospel that we have seen, what is the overall response to the gospel?*

3. *Why do you think Paul asked that Timothy and Silas join him as soon as possible in Athens?*

## DAY FIVE READING AND QUESTIONS

Reread the entire passage (Acts 17:1-15)

1. *Why do you think God-fearing Greeks were more open to embracing the good news about Jesus than were Jews?*

2. *If we were Jews would we be more like those of Thessalonica or Berea? In other words, would we be more tied to tradition or more open to searching the word?*

3. *Why did Paul consistently go first to the synagogues when he entered a new city?*

## MEDITATION

Acts 17 demonstrates Paul's amazing flexibility in preaching. It also gives us important insight into how he handled adversity. This lesson and the next will show us two radically different approaches to teaching the same message of salvation. Paul used one in the synagogue, where there was a deep respect for the Hebrew Scriptures. In our next study, Paul will be preaching in Athens, where the Greeks would have held in contempt anything written or spoken in Hebrew. Clearly, this would call for another course in teaching the story of redemption.

When in a synagogue, like the one in Thessalonica, Paul reasoned, explained, and provided proof that Jesus was indeed Messiah. Some Jews, many God-fearing Greeks as well as many prominent women believed as a result. As we now have come to expect, opposition quickly arose causing Paul to escape to Berea. Without slowing down, Paul went right to the synagogue and began reasoning, explaining and providing evidences that Jesus was the Christ. These Jews were noble God seekers. They received the message with great eagerness, and turned quickly to the Scriptures they knew well and found that what Paul was saying was indeed true. Many turned to God. The distracters again disrupted Paul's work, but God's kingdom was growing rapidly in spite of their efforts.

What can we learn from all of these incidents? People with open hearts gladly receive the message. But it is not a neutral message. People either embraced it with joy or violently refused it. Why did those who opposed Paul see his message as dangerous? Most of the tension in Acts is instigated by religious leaders who saw themselves as the exclusive children of God. They looked to a day when messiah would come and even make them more important. So when Paul proclaimed a Messiah that opened the doors of God's kingdom to all, including Gentiles, they could not tolerate his message.

The good news of the kingdom is for all who will hear it. May we never be on the side insisting that God's work is about us to the exclusion of others.

"Gracious God, thank you for salvation. May I never stand in the way of the proclamation of your truth!"

# PAUL IN ATHENS

## (ACTS 17:16-34)

### DAY ONE READING AND QUESTIONS

[16] While Paul was waiting for them in Athens, he was greatly distressed to see that the city was full of idols. [17] So he reasoned in the synagogue with the Jews and the God-fearing Greeks, as well as in the marketplace day by day with those who happened to be there. [18] A group of Epicurean and Stoic philosophers began to dispute with him. Some of them asked, "What is this babbler trying to say?" Others remarked, "He seems to be advocating foreign gods." They said this because Paul was preaching the good news about Jesus and the resurrection.

*1. Where did Paul first teach in Athens?*

*2. What was the content of his preaching in the marketplace?*

*3. Are we bold enough to speak about our faith in Jesus in places where ideas are exchanged in our culture?*

## DAY TWO READING AND QUESTIONS

[19] Then they took him and brought him to a meeting of the Areopagus, where they said to him, "May we know what this new teaching is that you are presenting? [20] You are bringing some strange ideas to our ears, and we want to know what they mean." [21] (All the Athenians and the foreigners who lived there spent their time doing nothing but talking about and listening to the latest ideas.) [22] Paul then stood up in the meeting of the Areopagus and said: "Men of Athens! I see that in every way you are very religious. [23] For as I walked around and looked carefully at your objects of worship, I even found an altar with this inscription: TO AN UNKNOWN GOD. Now what you worship as something unknown I am going to proclaim to you.

*1. What did Paul assume about the religion of the Athenians?*

*2. Why do you think Paul introduced his sermon with an appeal to the unknown god?*

*3. What does Paul's view of the Athenians teach us about how we should view those of other religious beliefs?*

## DAY THREE READING AND QUESTIONS

[24] "The God who made the world and everything in it is the Lord of heaven and earth and does not live in temples built by hands. [25] And he is not served by human hands, as if he needed anything, because he himself gives all men life and breath and everything else. [26] From one man he made every nation of men, that they should inhabit the whole earth; and he determined the times set for them and the exact

places where they should live. [27] God did this so that men would seek him and perhaps reach out for him and find him, though he is not far from each one of us. [28] 'For in him we live and move and have our being.' As some of your own poets have said, 'We are his offspring.' [29] "Therefore since we are God's offspring, we should not think that the divine being is like gold or silver or stone— an image made by man's design and skill. [30] In the past God overlooked such ignorance, but now he commands all people everywhere to repent. [31] For he has set a day when he will judge the world with justice by the man he has appointed. He has given proof of this to all men by raising him from the dead."

*1. How does Paul describe God in this teaching?*

*2. What does Paul demonstrate by quoting Greek poets?*

*3. What does this tell us about how we should approach teaching those of other faiths?*

## DAY FOUR READING AND QUESTIONS

[32] When they heard about the resurrection of the dead, some of them sneered, but others said, "We want to hear you again on this subject." [33] At that, Paul left the Council. [34] A few men became followers of Paul and believed. Among them was Dionysius, a member of the Areopagus, also a woman named Damaris, and a number of others.

*1. Why does mention of the resurrection evoke such a strong response?*

*2. What was the response to Paul's teaching?*

*3. Why do you think Luke mentions two of those who responded by name?*

## DAY FIVE READING AND QUESTIONS

Reread the entire passage (Acts 17:16-34)

*1. Why didn't Paul's distress over idolatry lead to contempt? What can we learn from this?*

*2. Can you remember a time when you dismissed someone as a candidate for God's kingdom because of their beliefs? If so, what can we learn from Paul concerning such people?*

*3. Are we prepared to present the gospel of Jesus Christ in any setting? What can we do to better prepare ourselves to present Jesus, for example, to Muslims?*

## MEDITATION

In the synagogues, Paul reasoned, explained and gave evidence that Jesus was the Christ. He used what they had in common—belief that the Hebrew Scriptures were the word of God. But when he began teaching in the marketplace, his "lesson plans" changed. While all of his teachings eventually led to Jesus as the Christ, Paul varied his approach according to the needs of those listening.

Though greatly distressed by the many idols in the city, he did not allow his feelings to lead to distain. Those in the marketplace ridiculed Paul as a babbler, and most likely took him to the Areopagus for entertainment. Even under these circumstances, Paul refused to allow his feelings to influence his teaching. What would we have done? If we found ourselves in a city full of idols and were made fun of because of our belief, and then given the opportunity to speak, what would we say?

Paul had no interest in vindicating himself. His deepest passion was to lead nonbelievers to new life in Jesus Christ. He understood that all of humanity was seeking God, but many were looking in the wrong places. Paul assumed the Athenians' belief in pagan gods was a genuine attempt to find the true God. We would do well to imitate Paul in this. We must not regard those who believe in other gods or religious systems as mindless or foolish. They, too, are children of God. They simply do not know it. They are seeking him but have not found him. It is our responsibility to let them see his face, which is exactly what Paul did.

Paul's presentation before the Areopagus is a magnificent sermon about the One, True God. He began with a point they discussed often— the idol erected to "the unknown god." Instead of attacking idolatry, he engaged them in a religious discussion that greatly interested them. Paul provided compelling reasons to believe in one God, a God above all gods. He spoke of a God so immense and transcendent that no work of human hands could contain or even begin to represent him. Yet the God of whom Paul spoke was so compassionate that he calls all to new life. While his discussion of the resurrection caused some to turn away, others were intrigued and wanted to hear more. Some came to belief, which is astounding when you consider the makeup of the group. What an amazing demonstration of the power of the Word of God to penetrate hearts that were so far away from the truth on so many fronts. Luke challenges us to realize that no one is beyond hope when the message of Jesus is presented in a meaningful and compassionate way that connects to his or her interests and questions.

"Heavenly Father, may we see those who believe differently than us as your children, even though we have profound disagreements with them. Use us as instruments to bring them to active faith in you."

# PAUL IN CORINTH

## (ACTS 18:1-17)

## DAY ONE READING AND QUESTIONS

[1] After this, Paul left Athens and went to Corinth. [2] There he met a Jew named Aquila, a native of Pontus, who had recently come from Italy with his wife Priscilla, because Claudius had ordered all the Jews to leave Rome. Paul went to see them, [3] and because he was a tentmaker as they were, he stayed and worked with them. [4] Every Sabbath he reasoned in the synagogue, trying to persuade Jews and Greeks.

*1. What do you think Luke mentions Paul forming a close friendship with Aquila and Priscilla?*

*2. What did Paul have in common with Aquila and Priscilla? What principle might we learn from Paul's working with them?*

*3. What was Paul's Sabbath activity?*

## DAY TWO READING AND QUESTIONS

[5] When Silas and Timothy came from Macedonia, Paul devoted himself exclusively to preaching, testifying to the Jews that Jesus was the Christ. [6] But when the Jews opposed Paul and became abusive, he shook out his clothes in protest and said to them, "Your blood be on your own heads! I am clear of my responsibility. From now on I will go to the Gentiles." [7] Then Paul left the synagogue and went next door to the house of Titius Justus, a worshiper of God.

> *1. What is meant by "preaching" in verse 5? How does this compare to today's use of the term?*

> *2. Why did Paul "shake out his clothes"?*

> *3. What would be a time when it might be justified to do as Paul and preach/teach in another location?*

## DAY THREE READING AND QUESTION

[8] Crispus, the synagogue ruler, and his entire household believed in the Lord; and many of the Corinthians who heard him believed and were baptized. [9] One night the Lord spoke to Paul in a vision: "Do not be afraid; keep on speaking, do not be silent. [10] For I am with you, and no one is going to attack and harm you, because I have many people in this city." [11] So Paul stayed for a year and a half, teaching them the word of God.

> *1. Did Paul's move to Titius Justus' house keep him from converting Jews? What does this tell us about his decision to leave the synagogue?*

*2. What was the purpose of God's message in Paul's vision?*

*3. What do you think Luke intended for us to gain from this episode in Paul's life?*

## DAY FOUR READING AND QUESTIONS

[02] While Gallio was proconsul of Achaia, the Jews made a united attack on Paul and brought him into court. [13] "This man," they charged, "is persuading the people to worship God in ways contrary to the law." [14] Just as Paul was about to speak, Gallio said to the Jews, "If you Jews were making a complaint about some misdemeanor or serious crime, it would be reasonable for me to listen to you. [15] But since it involves questions about words and names and your own law—settle the matter yourselves. I will not be a judge of such things." [16] So he had them ejected from the court. [17] Then they all turned on Sosthenes the synagogue ruler and beat him in front of the court. But Gallio showed no concern whatever.

*1. What happened next which made the vision particularly helpful?*

*2. Why would Gallio not hear the case against Paul?*

*3. Why do you think Sosthenes was beaten? What does Gallio's response to this show?*

## DAY FIVE READING AND QUESTIONS

Reread the entire passage (Acts 18:1-17)

*1. Have you experienced the reassurance of God while doing His work? If so, when and how?*

2. *What can we learn from Paul concerning ways to teach the good news of Jesus effectively?*

3. *What should we do when we are falsely accused or even persecuted?*

# MEDITATION

We know much about Corinth because of Paul's later correspondence to the church—and it all began with Paul's encounter with Priscilla and Aquila. Paul worked together with them making tents as he preached the good news of the gospel. Luke gives us a quick look at one way Paul supported his missions. He was not afraid to roll up his sleeves and work.

One more time Paul preached in the synagogue until opposition arose. When thrown out of the synagogue, he simply moved next door and kept right on preaching. Times would never be easy for Paul. While there were brief periods of relative calm in his life, most of the time he was battling nonbelievers while continuing to preach. The Lord blessed him with visions of reassurance, which were of great consolation to Paul. Luke records these words of comfort because he wants his readers to continue to experience God's strengthening reconfirmation. God's message to Paul is clear: "Keep on preaching—do not be silent." We need to hear these words. The Lord had a great number of people prepared to hear the good news there, and Paul was his mouthpiece.

As we might expect, persecution followed. The Jews were not satisfied with expelling Paul from the synagogue; they wanted him arrested by civil authorities. The Jewish leaders decided to take their case against Paul before Gallio. They accused him of persuading people to worship God in a manner contrary to their law. Paul was about to defend himself when Gallio dismissed the entire case as frivolous. The case so angered the Corinthians that they beat Sosthenes, the synagogue ruler who initiated the charge. Gallio demonstrated his contempt for the matter and the Jews with a total lack of concern for the treatment of Sosthenes. As the one in charge, Gallio indirectly vindicates Paul's teaching by not opposing it.

What was Luke's point in including this story? Remember Luke is writing to Theophilus. He wants to convince him that everything he has heard about Jesus is true. Every time Paul's enemies brought him before a court of law outside of Jewish control he was vindicated. The times Paul was beaten or flogged occurred because someone failed to observe Roman law. Opposition arose because of jealousy, an unwillingness to listen, or the desire to preserve one's self-interests.

We must believe that we are under the protection of God—that is, if we are about his work. That does not mean we will escape harm or even death. The Romans eventually executed Paul. Nonetheless, God will protect us until his work through us is completed. Hear the voice of God, "I am with you."

"Almighty God, give us the courage to trust you at all times, even when it seems everyone is against us."

# PRISCILLA, AQUILA, AND APOLLOS
## (ACTS 18:18-19:7)

### DAY ONE READING AND QUESTIONS

[18] Paul stayed on in Corinth for some time. Then he left the brothers and sailed for Syria, accompanied by Priscilla and Aquila. Before he sailed, he had his hair cut off at Cenchrea because of a vow

he had taken. [19] They arrived at Ephesus, where Paul left Priscilla and Aquila. He himself went into the synagogue and reasoned with the Jews. [20] When they asked him to spend more time with them, he declined. [21]But as he left, he promised, "I will come back if it is God's will." Then he set sail from Ephesus. [22] When he landed at Caesarea, he went up and greeted the church and then went down to Antioch. [23] After spending some time in Antioch, Paul set out from there and traveled from place to place throughout the region of Galatia and Phrygia, strengthening all the disciples.

*1. Why did Paul have his hair cut off?*

*2. What do you think "strengthening all the disciples" entailed?*

*3. What do you think Paul would tell you if he visited your church?*

## DAY TWO READING AND QUESTIONS

[24] Meanwhile a Jew named Apollos, a native of Alexandria, came to Ephesus. He was a learned man, with a thorough knowledge of the Scriptures. [25] He had been instructed in the way of the Lord, and he spoke with great fervor and taught about Jesus accurately, though he knew only the baptism of John. [26] He began to speak boldly in the synagogue. When Priscilla and Aquila heard him, they invited him to their home and explained to him the way of God more adequately.

*1. What are the "Scriptures" referred to in verse 24?*

*2. If Apollos only knew the baptism of John, how could he teach about Jesus accurately?*

*3. How did Priscilla and Aquila address the lack of knowledge on Apollo's part? What can we learn from this example?*

## DAY THREE READING AND QUESTIONS

[27] When Apollos wanted to go to Achaia, the brothers encouraged him and wrote to the disciples there to welcome him. On arriving, he was a great help to those who by grace had believed. [28] For he vigorously refuted the Jews in public debate, proving from the Scriptures that Jesus was the Christ.

*1. What does the work of Apollos show us concerning the continuing spread of the gospel?*

*2. How did he prove Jesus was the Christ?*

*3. What can we learn from the example of Apollos?*

## DAY FOUR READING AND QUESTIONS

[1] While Apollos was at Corinth, Paul took the road through the interior and arrived at Ephesus. There he found some disciples [2] and asked them, "Did you receive the Holy Spirit when you believed?" They answered, "No, we have not even heard that there is a Holy Spirit." [3] So Paul asked, "Then what baptism did you receive?" "John's baptism," they replied. [4] Paul said, "John's baptism was a baptism of repentance. He told the people to believe in the one coming after him, that is, in Jesus." [5] On hearing this, they were baptized into the name of the Lord Jesus. [6] When Paul placed his hands on them, the Holy Spirit came on them, and they spoke in tongues and prophesied. [7]There were about twelve men in all.

*1. What promise does Paul fulfill in 19:1?*

*2. How could there be disciples of Jesus who had not heard of the Holy Spirit?*

*3. When did these believers receive the Holy Spirit?*

## DAY FIVE READING AND QUESTIONS

Reread the entire passage (Acts 18:18-19:7)

*1. Are you surprised Apollos knew so much about Jesus even though he only knew of John's baptism?*

*2. Can you think of an individual reached with the gospel who in turn taught many others, who then also turned and taught others?*

*3. Diagram your own "kingdom tree". Who taught you? Do you know who taught the one who taught you? Who have you brought to Jesus? Who did those you helped convert bring to belief?*

## MEDITATION

When Paul decided it was time to leave Corinth, he headed for another great city in Asia Minor—Ephesus. But before he left, he made a vow (we don't know what or why) and cut his hair as a sign of commitment. Vows were very serious commitments for Jews. Remember that Paul never stopped being a Jew. He saw himself as a Jew who knew that the messiah had come and fulfilled all of God's promises. This did not bring his past religious practices to a halt—it brought them into the light of God's kingdom.

When Paul arrived at Ephesus, in the company of Aquila and Priscilla, he again heads to the synagogue. He then did something unusual. When asked to remain, he declined. He promised to return if it was the Lord's will. It seems he felt it was time to return to Antioch. Perhaps Paul recognized Ephesus could be another experience like that of Corinth—it would require a long stay. He wanted to make sure the young churches throughout Galatia and Phrygia were continuing to grow in spiritual maturity and fervor.

In the meantime, back in Ephesus, Luke gives us a picture of an active group of disciples. Apollos, a learned man, spoke boldly in the synagogue about Jesus. His message was compelling and powerful. However, he knew only of the baptism of John—a baptism of repentance—calling one to prepare for Jesus. Apollos knew the Scriptures well. He understood how it all pointed to Jesus. He was living in "the Way," though he did not know the full story.

It is heart warming and helpful to note how Priscilla and Aquila handled the situation. They did not publicly confront Apollos about his incomplete teaching. They invited him into their home and "explained to him the way of God more adequately. " As a result, Apollos become a significant figure in the rapid growth of the early church.

Consider the process that led Aquila and Priscilla to instruct Apollos. They first met Paul, worked with him and learned from him—then they traveled to Ephesus where Paul left them. There they met Apollos, and taught him. In turn, Apollos headed to Corinth and assisted in wonderful ways in building the churches in that area. Indeed, the kingdom is like a mustard seed. We never know what God will do with a good word spoken for him. But we do know this—he is at work in us just as he was in Paul.

Paul then has a similar experience as he fulfills his promise and returns to Ephesus. He instructed a group of believers in Jesus about the Holy Spirit, of whom they had not heard. Many with whom we interact daily may be in situations similar to that of Apollos and the group of believers Paul encountered in Ephesus. They love the Lord, but lack teaching. It is wrong to view such people as intentionally shunning the full truth of the gospel. Invite them home, talk to them of Jesus over a table of good food. Tell them of Jesus and his love for them. Demonstrate the grace of God's loving Holy Spirit. This is how the church grows.

"Loving Lord, teach me to respond to the needs of others with love and grace."

# PAUL IN EPHESUS

## (ACTS 19:8-41)

### DAY ONE READING AND QUESTIONS

[8] Paul entered the synagogue and spoke boldly there for three months, arguing persuasively about the kingdom of God. [9] But some of them became obstinate; they refused to believe and publicly maligned the Way. So Paul left them. He took the disciples with him and had discussions daily in the lecture hall of Tyrannus. [10] This went on for two years, so that all the Jews and Greeks who lived in the province of Asia heard the word of the Lord. [11] God did extraordinary miracles through Paul, [12] so that even handkerchiefs and aprons that had touched him were taken to the sick, and their illnesses were cured and the evil spirits left them.

*1. How long did Paul preach in the synagogue in Ephesus? Does this surprise you? Why?*

*2. Why do you think Paul's preaching was characterized as "the Way"? Would this be a good description for followers of Jesus Christ today?*

*3. Who does Luke point out as the one doing the miracles? Why is this significant for Luke?*

## DAY TWO READING AND QUESTIONS

[13] Some Jews who went around driving out evil spirits tried to invoke the name of the Lord Jesus over those who were demon-possessed. They would say, "In the name of Jesus, whom Paul preaches, I command you to come out." [14] Seven sons of Sceva, a Jewish chief priest, were doing this. [15] One day the evil spirit answered them, "Jesus I know, and I know about Paul, but who are you?" [16] Then the man who had the evil spirit jumped on them and overpowered them all. He gave them such a beating that they ran out of the house naked and bleeding. [17] When this became known to the Jews and Greeks living in Ephesus, they were all seized with fear, and the name of the Lord Jesus was held in high honor. [18] Many of those who believed now came and openly confessed their evil deeds. [19] A number who had practiced sorcery brought their scrolls together and burned them publicly. When they calculated the value of the scrolls, the total came to fifty thousand drachmas. [20] In this way the word of the Lord spread widely and grew in power.

*1. What does the story about the non-believing Jews using Jesus' name tell us about the power of his name?*

*2. Why did the beating of the sons of Sceva lead people to have an even deeper respect for the name of Jesus?*

*3. If we today were to experience a revival like that in Ephesus, openly confessing our idolatry, what do you think we would bring to Paul to be destroyed?*

## DAY THREE READING AND QUESTIONS

[21] After all this had happened, Paul decided to go to Jerusalem, passing through Macedonia and Achaia. "After I have been there," he said, "I must visit Rome also." [22] He sent two of his helpers, Timothy and Erastus, to Macedonia, while he stayed in the province of Asia a little longer. [23] About that time there arose a great disturbance about the Way. [24] A silversmith named Demetrius, who made silver shrines of Artemis, brought in no little business for the craftsmen. [25] He called them together, along with the workmen in related trades, and said: "Men, you know we receive a good income from this business. [26] And you see and hear how this fellow Paul has convinced and led astray large numbers of people here in Ephesus and in practically the whole province of Asia. He says that man-made gods are no gods at all. [27] There is danger not only that our trade will lose its good name, but also that the temple of the great goddess Artemis will be discredited, and the goddess herself, who is worshiped throughout the province of Asia and the world, will be robbed of her divine majesty." [28] When they heard this, they were furious and began shouting: "Great is Artemis of the Ephesians!"

*1. What does Demetrius' concern tell us about the success of Paul's preaching?*

*2. How does Demetrius try to hide his real concern (monetary loss) in order to stir up the crowd?*

*3. Have you experienced any similar situations where one tried to hide his or her real financial concerns under the guise of a religious concern? How was the situation handled?*

## DAY FOUR READING AND QUESTIONS

[29] Soon the whole city was in an uproar. The people seized Gaius and Aristarchus, Paul's traveling companions from Macedonia, and rushed as one man into the theater. [30] Paul wanted to appear before the crowd, but the disciples would not let him. [31] Even some of the officials of the province, friends of Paul, sent him a message begging him not to venture into the theater. [32] The assembly was in confusion: Some were shouting one thing, some another. Most of the people did not even know why they were there. [33] The Jews pushed Alexander to the front, and some of the crowd shouted instructions to him. He motioned for silence in order to make a defense before the people. [34] But when they realized he was a Jew, they all shouted in unison for about two hours: "Great is Artemis of the Ephesians!" [35] The city clerk quieted the crowd and said: "Men of Ephesus, doesn't all the world know that the city of Ephesus is the guardian of the temple of the great Artemis and of her image, which fell from heaven? [36] Therefore, since these facts are undeniable, you ought to be quiet and not do anything rash. [37] You have brought these men here, though they have neither robbed temples nor blasphemed our goddess. [38] If, then, Demetrius and his fellow craftsmen have a grievance against anybody, the courts are open and there are proconsuls. They can press charges. [39] If there is anything further you want to bring up, it must be settled in a legal assembly. [40] As it is, we are in danger of being charged with rioting because of today's events. In that case we would not be able to

account for this commotion, since there is no reason for it." [41] After he had said this, he dismissed the assembly.

1. *Why would the province officials try to keep Paul from appearing in the theater? What does this tell us of Paul's status among the officials of that province?*

2. *Why were most of the people there? What does this tell us about human nature?*

3. *What does the response of the city clerk tell us about how he understood the teaching of "the Way?"*

## DAY FIVE READING AND QUESTIONS

Reread the entire passage (Acts 19:8-41)

1. *Why do you think the gospel was so well received at Ephesus?*

2. *Does the gospel still have the power to change entire pagan cultures? In what way is our current culture "pagan"?*

3. *Dream a little. Try to envision a way of evoking a belief movement so strong that it would threaten the collapse of certain godless industries. How could such a thing happen?*

## MEDITATION

Yet again we see "the Way" as the identifier of those following Jesus. While Luke informed us earlier that some called believers

"Christians," it is significant that he chose not to use that term. In fact, "Christian" is only used three times in the entire New Testament. Luke uses the description "the Way" at least nine times in Acts. "The Way" demonstrates that life in Jesus is not a static set of religious practices but a dynamic path of life initiated by Jesus. It is a life of authentic and committed discipleship to Jesus Christ.

In Ephesus, Paul was able to preach in the synagogue for three full months. This is unexpected, especially in view of his former experiences in synagogues. Normally, he was cast out within a few days, but apparently the Jews in Ephesus were more open to hear the gospel. Even when some in the synagogue became obstinate, Paul simply moved his daily discussions to a lecture hall—and continued teaching for two years. This is a golden time for the expansion of the early church in Acts. How exciting it must have been!

The "sons of Sceva" episode must have delighted Luke. Reading between the lines, you sense Luke's smile as he wrote. We would expect others to try to cash in on the success and power of Paul. Those who were not working with a sincere heart, however, did not have God's blessings. This was no magic show, as the sons of Sceva soon learned. Through this event, the name of Jesus was even more highly honored than before. Former sorcerers recognized the superior power of Paul through Jesus and not only repented and believed, but destroyed many valuable scrolls on sorcery.

Paul's teaching was so effective he disrupted the city's commerce. Those making idols were losing money. People were turning to God at such a pace that false beliefs were failing. This event brings up an interesting thought. Can you imagine believing in a goddess of such little power that she could lose her divine majesty through the preaching of one man? Nonetheless, this idea, proposed by Demetrius the silversmith, incited a riot. The commotion led the rioters into the large town theater. Though Paul badly wanted to speak to the crowd (are we surprised?), it was not the place to expound on the gospel. As is often the case with riotous crowds, many had no idea what they were protesting. Once again, Paul was vindicated—this time by the mayor— as he reminded the crowd their behavior was illegal.

We need to pay special attention to what Paul was not doing in all this commotion. While he was clearly teaching about the One True God, he was not ridiculing the pagans' belief. This would not only have been unnecessary, but also needlessly inflammatory. The profession of faith in Jesus need not involve the ridiculing of another's belief. Let truth stand as truth. It is powerful enough to defeat any false belief.

"Lord of truth, help us to stand on the truth of your word and not resort to ridiculing the beliefs of those who oppose us."

# PAUL IN TROAS AND BEYOND
## (ACTS 20:1-16)

### DAY ONE READING AND QUESTIONS

[1] When the uproar had ended, Paul sent for the disciples and, after encouraging them, said good-by and set out for Macedonia. [2] He traveled through that area, speaking many words of encouragement to the people, and finally arrived in Greece, [3] where he stayed three months. Because the Jews made a plot against him just as he was about to sail for Syria, he decided to go back through Macedonia.

*1. Why do you think Paul is so involved in constantly encouraging the believers?*

*. Why do the constant dangers Paul finds himself in not seem to deter him?*

*3. Do you feel the same sense of purpose and determination when you encounter difficulty or danger because of your belief in Jesus Christ? Why or why not?*

## DAY TWO READING AND QUESTIONS

[4] He was accompanied by Sopater son of Pyrrhus from Berea, Aristarchus and Secundus from Thessalonica, Gaius from Derbe, Timothy also, and Tychicus and Trophimus from the province of Asia. [5] These men went on ahead and waited for us at Troas. [6] But we sailed from Philippi after the Feast of Unleavened Bread, and five days later joined the others at Troas, where we stayed seven days.

*1. Why do you think Luke provides the names of Paul's companions?*

*2. Why do you think Luke provides so much detail in terms of where Paul went and how many days he stayed in one place?*

*3. What does Luke's reference to the Feast of Unleavened Bread tell you about Paul and his observation of the Jewish feast days?*

## DAY THREE READING AND QUESTIONS

[7] On the first day of the week we came together to break bread. Paul spoke to the people and, because he intended to leave the next day, kept on talking until midnight. [8] There were many lamps in the upstairs room where we were meeting. [9] Seated in a window was a

young man named Eutychus, who was sinking into a deep sleep as Paul talked on and on. When he was sound asleep, he fell to the ground from the third story and was picked up dead. [10] Paul went down, threw himself on the young man and put his arms around him. "Don't be alarmed," he said. "He's alive!" [11] Then he went upstairs again and broke bread and ate. After talking until daylight, he left. [12]The people took the young man home alive and were greatly comforted.

1. *What was the purpose of the gathering at Troas?*

2. *Describe the assembly of believers. What did they do and for how long did they meet?*

3. *What were the believers doing when they broke bread together?*

4. *How do church assemblies today reflect what the church of Troas did when they came together?*

## DAY FOUR READING AND QUESTIONS

[13] We went on ahead to the ship and sailed for Assos, where we were going to take Paul aboard. He had made this arrangement because he was going there on foot. [14] When he met us at Assos, we took him aboard and went on to Mitylene. [15] The next day we set sail from there and arrived off Kios. The day after that we crossed over to Samos, and on the following day arrived at Miletus. [16] Paul had decided to sail past Ephesus to avoid spending time in the province of Asia, for he was in a hurry to reach Jerusalem, if possible, by the day of Pentecost.

1. *Why did Paul hurry past Ephesus?*

*2. Why do you think Paul wanted to be in Jerusalem for Pentecost?*

*3. Clearly, the Spirit was active in guiding Paul. Here, it seems, Paul was setting his own travel agenda. How can Paul's travel plans enlighten us as we make decisions on how to use our time and make choices on where we should go to help expand the kingdom?*

## DAY FIVE READING AND QUESTIONS

Reread the entire passage (Acts 20:1-16)

*1. If you were Eutychus, how do you think you would remember the night of Paul's visit?*

*2. What do you think Paul was discussing with the church at Troas for all of those hours?*

*3. Do you think of Paul as a great encourager of the saints? What do you think he would say to your church if he came for a visit?*

## MEDITATION

Paul had a great desire to make it to Jerusalem for Pentecost, but he waited several days in Troas so that he could meet with the believers there. Because Paul had to depart the next day, he dialogued with them until midnight. Not everyone was able to endure the long discussion—poor Eutychus! Most of us can at least identify with him. Fortunately, if we fall asleep in church we are not in a position to hurt ourselves. I doubt Eutychus ever forgot that day. Falling to his death, he was raised to sit at the table of the Lord once again. This was not a simple passing of an unleavened cracker and a small sip of grape juice. Paul had already spoken nearly six hours, and would continue to discuss the Lord with them until daybreak. While this was the "breaking of the bread" in remembrance of Jesus, it was within the context of a full meal together. Some communities of faith in today's world have made a conscious effort to recover the rich heritage of table fellowship—brothers and sisters gathered for the purpose of eating together and "breaking bread" in that setting. Discussions around the meal table are much different from discussions when seated formally in worship services. The Lord comes alive at his feast table when his disciples come together in order hear of his work in the lives of fellow believers.

This is a fascinating glimpse of the early church. They met for at least ten hours. They studied at Paul's feet, listening to his testimony, marveling at the powerful work of the Lord. They paused to eat together, nourishing their bodies, but more importantly remembering the presence of the Lord at their table—renewing their covenant to be the image of God to the world. They just could not get enough of what Paul was teaching. They knew he would be leaving, so they kept listening, asking questions, and Paul kept teaching and encouraging. What a wonderful feast our brothers and sisters at Troas enjoyed that memorable night. What a joy to be a part of the kingdom of God—where all is in anticipation of the eternal feast to come!

Come, sit at the Lord's table and enjoy the feast—the feast of relationship with God and his people. Talk to one another about his wonderful love and his work in your life. Gather to celebrate, to feast, to learn, to remember, to praise the One who made you an intricate part of this marvelous story.

"Lord, thank you for your gracious invitation to your table. May I never take for granted the blessings that await me there."

# A MESSAGE FROM PAUL'S HEART

## (ACTS 20:17-38)

### DAY ONE READING AND QUESTIONS

[17] From Miletus, Paul sent to Ephesus for the elders of the church. [18]When they arrived, he said to them: "You know how I lived the whole time I was with you, from the first day I came into the province of Asia. [19] I served the Lord with great humility and with tears, although I was severely tested by the plots of the Jews. [20] You know that I have not hesitated to preach anything that would be helpful to you but have taught you publicly and from house to house. [21] I have declared to both Jews and Greeks that they must turn to God in repentance and have faith in our Lord Jesus.

*1. Based on Paul's previous work with disciples and churches, why do you think he called for the elders from Ephesus?*

*2. Why do you think Paul called attention to the way he had lived among them?*

*3. Do we preach today the essence of what Paul preached in Ephesus?*

## DAY TWO READING AND QUESTIONS

[22] "And now, compelled by the Spirit, I am going to Jerusalem, not knowing what will happen to me there. [23] I only know that in every city the Holy Spirit warns me that prison and hardships are facing me. [24] However, I consider my life worth nothing to me, if only I may finish the race and complete the task the Lord Jesus has given me— the task of testifying to the gospel of God's grace. [25] "Now I know that none of you among whom I have gone about preaching the kingdom will ever see me again. [26] Therefore, I declare to you today that I am innocent of the blood of all men. [27] For I have not hesitated to proclaim to you the whole will of God.

1. *Why did the Spirit both compel Paul to go to Jerusalem but also warn him about what was to come?*

2. *What was the value of Paul's life, from his own perspective?*

3. *How do we view our lives in terms of what makes them valuable? What can we learn from Paul about how to value our lives?*

## DAY THREE READING AND QUESTIONS

[28] Keep watch over yourselves and all the flock of which the Holy Spirit has made you overseers. Be shepherds of the church of God, which he bought with his own blood. [29] I know that after I leave, savage wolves will come in among you and will not spare the flock. [30] Even from your own number men will arise and distort the truth in order to draw away disciples after them. [31] So be on your guard! Remember that for three years I never stopped warning each of you night and day with tears.

1. *Who did Paul believe appointed the elders?*

2. *What did Paul charge the elders to do?*

3. *What do you think Paul would say to the elders or leaders of your congregation if he visited them today?*

## DAY FOUR READING AND QUESTIONS

[32] "Now I commit you to God and to the word of his grace, which can build you up and give you an inheritance among all those who are sanctified. [33] I have not coveted anyone's silver or gold or clothing. [34]You yourselves know that these hands of mine have supplied my own needs and the needs of my companions. [35] In everything I did, I showed you that by this kind of hard work we must help the weak, remembering the words the Lord Jesus himself said: 'It is more blessed to give than to receive.'" [36] When he had said this, he knelt down with all of them and prayed. [37] They all wept as they embraced him and kissed him. [38] What grieved them most was his statement that they would never see his face again. Then they accompanied him to the ship.

1. *To what did Paul commit the elders and why did he do so?*

2. *What did Paul do with the elders before he left them? What does their response to his charge show us about the relationship Paul had with these elders?*

3. *What can we do to restore this kind of deep fellowship in our churches?*

176

## DAY FIVE READING AND QUESTIONS

Reread the entire passage (Acts 20:17-38)

*1. What do you think was the main burden on Paul's heart as he spoke with the elders from Ephesus?*

*2. Is it wise to use one's own example when speaking of the truth of the kingdom? Why or why not?*

*3. If you knew you were not going to see your most beloved friends again on this earth, what would you tell them before leaving?*

# MEDITATION

The Holy Spirit was compelling Paul to go to Jerusalem, and at the same time warning him of hostile treatment and imprisonment he would receive there. Though in a hurry to get to Jerusalem by Pentecost, Paul could not leave Asia without one last encounter with the elders of the church in Ephesus. He had spent much time in that city, and felt the deep need to encourage the shepherds of that church one more time. This brief picture allows us to look deeply into Paul's heart and see his passion for God and his church.

After declaring the heart of the gospel, Paul turned to his own situation. He wanted the Ephesians to know that he was not walking blindly into trouble. The Holy Spirit had warned Paul what was about to happen. Paul wanted the brothers and sisters in Ephesus to know his impending treatment was not because God had abandoned him. His own life, in and of itself, meant nothing to him—he only wanted to do what God desired. Oh, that we could embrace such a view of life! So many of us claim belief in God and Jesus, but are not willing to put ourselves at risk for the kingdom. Paul was not carelessly throwing his life away—he was being faithful. He knew God was able to keep that which he committed to him. There was no place for fear in his understanding of life in God's care.

The deep love that Paul had for these brethren is evident throughout this tender scene. He knew his ability to move freely and encourage his brothers would soon end. He desperately wanted them to remain faithful and continue to be active in the kingdom. Indeed, they would not meet again on this side of eternity. However, there will be an eternity for them to revisit those precious hours.

"Loving Father, thank you for the encouragement we receive from others in your kingdom. We look forward with great anticipation to the day when there will be no more parting or sorrow."

# PAUL IN JERUSALEM
## (ACTS 21:1-26)

### DAY ONE READING AND QUESTIONS

¹ After we had torn ourselves away from them, we put out to sea and sailed straight to Cos. The next day we went to Rhodes and from there to Patara. ² We found a ship crossing over to Phoenicia, went on board and set sail. ³ After sighting Cyprus and passing to the south of it, we sailed on to Syria. We landed at Tyre, where our ship was to

unload its cargo. [4] Finding the disciples there, we stayed with them seven days. Through the Spirit they urged Paul not to go on to Jerusalem. [5] But when our time was up, we left and continued on our way. All the disciples and their wives and children accompanied us out of the city, and there on the beach we knelt to pray. [6] After saying good-by to each other, we went aboard the ship, and they returned home. [7] We continued our voyage from Tyre and landed at Ptolemais, where we greeted the brothers and stayed with them for a day.

*1. Why do you think Luke describes Paul's group leaving the Ephesian elders as "tearing ourselves away" from them?*

*2. Why would the brethren at Tyre urge Paul "through the Spirit" not to go to Jerusalem?*

*3. What image of the church comes to mind as Paul and his band travel from port to port, encountering groups of believers?*

## DAY TWO READING AND QUESTIONS

[8] Leaving the next day, we reached Caesarea and stayed at the house of Philip the evangelist, one of the Seven. [9] He had four unmarried daughters who prophesied. [10] After we had been there a number of days, a prophet named Agabus came down from Judea. [11] Coming over to us, he took Paul's belt, tied his own hands and feet with it and said, "The Holy Spirit says, 'In this way the Jews of Jerusalem will bind the owner of this belt and will hand him over to the Gentiles.'" [12] When we heard this, we and the people there pleaded with Paul not to go up to Jerusalem. [13] Then Paul answered, "Why are you weeping and breaking my heart? I am ready not only to be bound, but also to die in Jerusalem for the name of the Lord Jesus." [15] The next day we set sail from there and

arrived off Kios. The day after that we crossed over to Samos, and on the following day arrived at Miletus. [16] Paul had decided to sail past Ephesus to avoid spending time in the province of Asia, for he was in a hurry to reach Jerusalem, if possible, by the day of Pentecost.

> *1. Why do you think the Holy Spirit was so active in warning Paul about what was to come?*

> *2. What was Paul's resolve in the face of impending danger?*

> *3. How do you think you would respond to such warnings from God about your journey with him?*

## DAY THREE READING AND QUESTIONS

[17] When we arrived at Jerusalem, the brothers received us warmly. [18] The next day Paul and the rest of us went to see James, and all the elders were present. [19] Paul greeted them and reported in detail what God had done among the Gentiles through his ministry. [20] When they heard this, they praised God. Then they said to Paul: "You see, brother, how many thousands of Jews have believed, and all of them are zealous for the law. [21] They have been informed that you teach all the Jews who live among the Gentiles to turn away from Moses, telling them not to circumcise their children or live according to our customs. [22] What shall we do? They will certainly hear that you have come, [23] so do what we tell you. There are four men with us who have made a vow. [24] Take these men, join in their purification rites and pay their expenses, so that they can have their heads shaved. Then everybody will know there is no truth in these reports about you, but that you yourself are living in obedience to the law. [25] As for the Gentile believers, we have written to them our decision that they should

abstain from food sacrificed to idols, from blood, from the meat of strangled animals and from sexual immorality."

> *1. What had been happening in Jerusalem as Paul had traveled throughout the Gentile lands?*
>
> *2. Why do you think the leaders in the church asked Paul to participate in the purification rites and to pay the expenses for him and four others?*
>
> *3. What are the leaders of the church in Jerusalem affirming by their statement concerning their letter to the Gentiles?*

## DAY FOUR READING AND QUESTIONS

[26] The next day Paul took the men and purified himself along with them. Then he went to the temple to give notice of the date when the days of purification would end and the offering would be made for each of them.

> *1. Why do you think Paul went along with the leaders' request?*
>
> *2. Can you think of a time in your experience when leaders attempted to settle potential conflict with a similar strategy?*

## DAY FIVE READING AND QUESTIONS

Reread the entire passage (Acts 21:1-26)

> *1. Why do think Paul had so much courage and resolve? How can we*

*develop that same sense of God's presence in our lives?*

*2. Is it possible for us to live without fear? How?*

*3. Why were the elders concerned about Paul's arrival in Jerusalem? Do you think they were right in asking him to do what they asked? Why or why not?*

## MEDITATION

Why would the Spirit direct Paul to go to Jerusalem, but also have believers warn him of his impending imprisonment? Luke wants us to know that Paul, just as Jesus, knew exactly what was about to happen to him. By warning the believers, the Spirit was preparing them for Paul's arrest. We see Paul's passion and love as Agabus plainly tells of his imminent arrest. As the brothers and sisters begged him not to go on, Paul pleaded with them to stop, for they were "breaking his heart." But he, like Jesus before him, would not be deterred. If need be, he was willing to die. His words remind us of Gethsemane, "The Lord's will be done." Jesus is indeed alive in his church.

Why do you suppose Paul went immediately to the elders when he arrived in Jerusalem? This is clearly where his heart was—he loved the church. He wanted to encourage them with words about God's gracious and exciting work in lands far away. Unfortunately, not all was well in the church. While there was the good news of many new converts in Jerusalem, the elders were concerned that many were opposed to Paul because they felt he was teaching against the Law of Moses. The elders wanted him to participate in a cleansing ritual that would demonstrate to all that Paul was still obedient to the law. Was this a good idea?

Conspicuously absent is any mention of the Holy Spirit in this decision process. Luke may have wanted us to know this was a human attempt to head off a problem. Paul chose to go along with their idea, which tells us of his humble and obedient heart. As we might have guessed, the ploy did not work. Attempts to pacify wrong thinking through symbolic gestures rarely succeed. The real problem was not that Paul was living in a way contrary to the law. Rather, his association with Gentiles was what disturbed his fellow Jews. He was eating and fellowshipping with Gentiles. Stated accusations are rarely the real problem in religious conflicts. If the issue really was one of not following the law, Paul could have easily demonstrated his faithfulness to the law. Luke has gone out of his way to show that Paul continued to practice his Jewish faith with vigor. As with Jesus, it was not so much what Paul did "religiously"; it was more about whom he invited to sit at his table.

"God of peace, give us wisdom to resolve our conflicts. Teach us how to confront wrongful attitudes in a way that allows you to bring repentance and restore peace."

# A RIOT AT THE TEMPLE
## (ACTS 21:27-22:29)

## DAY ONE READING AND QUESTIONS

[27] When the seven days were nearly over, some Jews from the province of Asia saw Paul at the temple. They stirred up the whole crowd and seized him, [28] shouting, "Men of Israel, help us! This is the man who teaches all men everywhere against our people and our law

and this place. And besides, he has brought Greeks into the temple area and defiled this holy place." [29] (They had previously seen Trophimus the Ephesian in the city with Paul and assumed that Paul had brought him into the temple area.) [30] The whole city was aroused, and the people came running from all directions. Seizing Paul, they dragged him from the temple, and immediately the gates were shut. [31] While they were trying to kill him, news reached the commander of the Roman troops that the whole city of Jerusalem was in an uproar. [32] He at once took some officers and soldiers and ran down to the crowd. When the rioters saw the commander and his soldiers, they stopped beating Paul. [33] The commander came up and arrested him and ordered him to be bound with two chains. Then he asked who he was and what he had done. [34] Some in the crowd shouted one thing and some another, and since the commander could not get at the truth because of the uproar, he ordered that Paul be taken into the barracks. [35] When Paul reached the steps, the violence of the mob was so great he had to be carried by the soldiers. [36] The crowd that followed kept shouting, "Away with him!"

1. *Why were these accusations leveled against Paul? What had he done to provoke such anger?*

2. *What was the crowd trying to do with Paul? Who rescued him?*

3. *Of what does this crowd remind you from the gospels?*

## DAY TWO READING AND QUESTIONS

[37] As the soldiers were about to take Paul into the barracks, he asked the commander, "May I say something to you?" "Do you speak Greek?" he replied. [38] "Aren't you the Egyptian who started a revolt

and led four thousand terrorists out into the desert some time ago?" [39]Paul answered, "I am a Jew, from Tarsus in Cilicia, a citizen of no ordinary city. Please let me speak to the people." [40] Having received the commander's permission, Paul stood on the steps and motioned to the crowd. When they were all silent, he said to them in Aramaic: [22:1] "Brothers and fathers, listen now to my defense." [2] When they heard him speak to them in Aramaic, they became very quiet. Then Paul said: [3] "I am a Jew, born in Tarsus of Cilicia, but brought up in this city. Under Gamaliel I was thoroughly trained in the law of our fathers and was just as zealous for God as any of you are today. [4] I persecuted the followers of this Way to their death, arresting both men and women and throwing them into prison, [5] as also the high priest and all the Council can testify. I even obtained letters from them to their brothers in Damascus, and went there to bring these people as prisoners to Jerusalem to be punished. [6] "About noon as I came near Damascus, suddenly a bright light from heaven flashed around me. [7] I fell to the ground and heard a voice say to me, 'Saul! Saul! Why do you persecute me?' [8] "'Who are you, Lord?' I asked. "'I am Jesus of Nazareth, whom you are persecuting,' he replied. [9] My companions saw the light, but they did not understand the voice of him who was speaking to me. [10] "'What shall I do, Lord?' I asked. "'Get up,' the Lord said, 'and go into Damascus. There you will be told all that you have been assigned to do.' [11] My companions led me by the hand into Damascus, because the brilliance of the light had blinded me.

*1. Why do you think Paul wanted to speak to the crowd trying to lynch him?*

*2. Why does Paul tell his story of conversion to the crowd?*

*3. What was Paul's attitude towards his accusers? What can we learn from Paul on this?*

## DAY THREE READING AND QUESTIONS

[12] "A man named Ananias came to see me. He was a devout observer of the law and highly respected by all the Jews living there. [13] He stood beside me and said, 'Brother Saul, receive your sight!' And at that very moment I was able to see him. [14] "Then he said: 'The God of our fathers has chosen you to know his will and to see the Righteous One and to hear words from his mouth. [15] You will be his witness to all men of what you have seen and heard. [16] And now what are you waiting for? Get up, be baptized and wash your sins away, calling on his name.' [17] "When I returned to Jerusalem and was praying at the temple, I fell into a trance [18] and saw the Lord speaking. 'Quick!' he said to me. 'Leave Jerusalem immediately, because they will not accept your testimony about me.' [19] "'Lord,' I replied, 'these men know that I went from one synagogue to another to imprison and beat those who believe in you. [20] And when the blood of your martyr Stephen was shed, I stood there giving my approval and guarding the clothes of those who were killing him.' [21] "Then the Lord said to me, 'Go; I will send you far away to the Gentiles.'"

  1. *Whose action does Paul emphasize throughout his telling of his story? Why is this important?*

  2. *Do you think those listening were familiar with Paul's story at all?*

  3. *Paul was called to be a witness of all he had seen and heard. Are we similarly called to witness to what God has done for us? If so, how should we do this?*

## DAY FOUR READING AND QUESTIONS

[22] The crowd listened to Paul until he said this. Then they raised their voices and shouted, "Rid the earth of him! He's not fit to live!" [23] As they were shouting and throwing off their cloaks and flinging dust into the air, [24] the commander ordered Paul to be taken into the barracks. He directed that he be flogged and questioned in order to find out why the people were shouting at him like this. [25] As they stretched him out to flog him, Paul said to the centurion standing there, "Is it legal for you to flog a Roman citizen who hasn't even been found guilty?" [26] When the centurion heard this, he went to the commander and reported it. "What are you going to do?" he asked. "This man is a Roman citizen." [27] The commander went to Paul and asked, "Tell me, are you a Roman citizen?" "Yes, I am," he answered. [28] Then the commander said, "I had to pay a big price for my citizenship." "But I was born a citizen," Paul replied. [29] Those who were about to question him withdrew immediately. The commander himself was alarmed when he realized that he had put Paul, a Roman citizen, in chains.

*1. What was it that Paul said that incited the crowd to riot?*

*2. Why was the commander going to flog Paul? What does this tell you of his normal treatment of those who disturbed the peace?*

*3. Why did Paul's questioners suddenly withdraw?*

## DAY FIVE READING AND QUESTIONS

Reread the entire passage (Acts 21:27-22:29)

1. *What impresses you most about Paul in this story?*

2. *Do you think Paul's Roman citizenship was a part of God's provi-dential care for him?*

3. *What have you been given that might be seen as a special gift from God to help you share the gospel of Jesus?*

## MEDITATION

There is sad irony in this story. The elders wanted people to see Paul at the temple piously worshiping God. Indeed, the Jews saw him in the temple area, but rather than acknowledging his piety, they falsely accused him of desecrating the temple. Their hatred of Gentiles was so deep that all they had to do was see Paul in Jerusalem with a Gentile to assume Paul had taken him into the temple. Inciting a riot by calling out, "Men of Israel, help us! This man has brought Greeks into the temple area," they attempted to kill Paul.

What caused such a violent reaction? The Jews of Paul's day were confident that God's work was all about them—to the exclusion of all others. They alone were God's chosen people. Therefore, they piously hated Gentiles. Do you catch how awkward that sounds—piously hated? While it is easy to condemn them for their narrow view of God's love, perhaps we should ask, "Are we guilty of the same sin?" It is a dangerous thing to believe that God has done all his work just for us. Do we not realize all people are God's children? Unfortunately, many people do not know who they are. If we are God's people, it is not for us to celebrate our good fortune while the rest of God's children perish around us, but for us to proclaim life in Jesus Christ so they, too, might claim their identity in him.

Undoubtedly, the crowd would have killed Paul had it not been for God's intervention through the Roman commander. Predictably, Paul desperately wanted to speak to those who wanted him dead. The crowd quieted and unexpectedly allowed him to speak. By now we should be able to anticipate what he would say—it is the story we have heard before. Paul told his listeners he was as zealous for God as they were. Just as in Athens, Paul did not question their love or zeal for God; he did not accuse them of deliberate wrongful behavior. He credited them with the desire to do right. He wanted them to hear that the God they sought and in whom they believed had miraculously intervened to change the direction of his life—and would do the same for them if they would repent.

Paul's mention of God's love for Gentiles ended the brief peace. In a scene reminiscent of Jesus' trial and of Stephen's stoning, they threw off their outer garments and called for Paul's death. Because he spoke of God's love for all, not just for the "chosen ones," those listening determined Paul was no longer fit to live.

What is most significant for us in this story is that in the midst of all this confusion, there was one man at peace. Paradoxically, he should be the one most distraught. After all, his life was at risk. Yet again, images of Jesus come to mind. How could Paul remain at peace in the midst of false accusations and death threats? How could Jesus allow those around him to commit such atrocities against him? How could Stephen possibly ask God to forgive those killing him? All of these heroes of faith knew what we often forget: God is sovereign and at work in all circumstances. His faithful children wait on him.

"Sovereign Lord, in the storms of my life teach me to wait on you. Calm my troubled spirit with the remembrance of your love for me."

# THE SANHEDRIN PLOTS AGAINST PAUL

## (ACTS 22:30-23:35)

### DAY ONE READING AND QUESTIONS

[30] The next day, since the commander wanted to find out exactly why Paul was being accused by the Jews, he released him and ordered the chief priests and all the Sanhedrin to assemble. Then he brought Paul and had him stand before them. [23:1] Paul looked straight at the Sanhedrin and said, "My brothers, I have fulfilled my duty to God in all good conscience to this day." [2] At this the high priest Ananias ordered those standing near Paul to strike him on the mouth. [3] Then Paul said to him, "God will strike you, you whitewashed wall! You sit there to judge me according to the law, yet you yourself violate the law by commanding that I be struck!" [4] Those who were standing near Paul said, "You dare to insult God's high priest?" [5] Paul replied, "Brothers, I did not realize that he was the high priest; for it is written: 'Do not speak evil about the ruler of your people.'"

*1. Why did the commander set up a meeting with Paul and the Sanhedrin?*

*2. Why do you think Ananias had Paul struck?*

*3. Why was Paul so quick to repent when he found out Ananias was the high priest? What can we learn from Paul in this?*

## DAY TWO READING AND QUESTIONS

[6] Then Paul, knowing that some of them were Sadducees and the others Pharisees, called out in the Sanhedrin, "My brothers, I am a Pharisee, the son of a Pharisee. I stand on trial because of my hope in the resurrection of the dead." [7] When he said this, a dispute broke out between the Pharisees and the Sadducees, and the assembly was divided. [8] (The Sadducees say that there is no resurrection, and that there are neither angels nor spirits, but the Pharisees acknowledge them all.) [9] There was a great uproar, and some of the teachers of the law who were Pharisees stood up and argued vigorously. "We find nothing wrong with this man," they said. "What if a spirit or an angel has spoken to him?" [10] The dispute became so violent that the commander was afraid Paul would be torn to pieces by them. He ordered the troops to go down and take him away from them by force and bring him into the barracks. [11] The following night the Lord stood near Paul and said, "Take courage! As you have testified about me in Jerusalem, so you must also testify in Rome."

*1. Why did Paul choose to begin his defense stating his belief in the resurrection?*

*2. What do you think the commander thought as violence broke out again?*

*3. Was God at work even in the midst of such violent misbehavior? If so, how?*

## DAY THREE READING AND QUESTIONS

[12] The next morning the Jews formed a conspiracy and bound themselves with an oath not to eat or drink until they had killed Paul. [13]More than forty men were involved in this plot. [14] They went to the chief priests and elders and said, "We have taken a solemn oath not to eat anything until we have killed Paul. [15] Now then, you and the Sanhedrin petition the commander to bring him before you on the pretext of wanting more accurate information about his case. We are ready to kill him before he gets here." [16] But when the son of Paul's sister heard of this plot, he went into the barracks and told Paul. [17]Then Paul called one of the centurions and said, "Take this young man to the commander; he has something to tell him." [18] So he took him to the commander. The centurion said, "Paul, the prisoner, sent for me and asked me to bring this young man to you because he has something to tell you." [19] The commander took the young man by the hand, drew him aside and asked, "What is it you want to tell me?" [20] He said: "The Jews have agreed to ask you to bring Paul before the Sanhedrin tomorrow on the pretext of wanting more accurate information about him. [21] Don't give in to them, because more than forty of them are waiting in ambush for him. They have taken an oath not to eat or drink until they have killed him. They are ready now, waiting for your consent to their request." [22] The commander dismissed the young man and cautioned him, "Don't tell anyone that you have reported this to me."

1. *Why do you think the Jews were so intent on killing Paul?*

2. *What does the foiled plot of the Jews demonstrate about how God's will is done?*

3. *What do you think Luke wants us to learn from Paul in this story?*

## DAY FOUR READING AND QUESTIONS

<sup>23</sup> Then he called two of his centurions and ordered them, "Get ready a detachment of two hundred soldiers, seventy horsemen and two hundred spearmen to go to Caesarea at nine tonight. <sup>24</sup> Provide mounts for Paul so that he may be taken safely to Governor Felix." <sup>25</sup>He wrote a letter as follows: <sup>26</sup> Claudius Lysias, To His Excellency, Governor Felix: Greetings. <sup>27</sup> This man was seized by the Jews and they were about to kill him, but I came with my troops and rescued him, for I had learned that he is a Roman citizen. <sup>28</sup> I wanted to know why they were accusing him, so I brought him to their Sanhedrin. <sup>29</sup> I found that the accusation had to do with questions about their law, but there was no charge against him that deserved death or imprisonment. <sup>30</sup> When I was informed of a plot to be carried out against the man, I sent him to you at once. I also ordered his accusers to present to you their case against him. <sup>31</sup> So the soldiers, carrying out their orders, took Paul with them during the night and brought him as far as Antipatris. <sup>32</sup> The next day they let the cavalry go on with him, while they returned to the barracks. <sup>33</sup> When the cavalry arrived in Caesarea, they delivered the letter to the governor and handed Paul over to him. <sup>34</sup> The governor read the letter and asked what province he was from. Learning that he was from Cilicia, <sup>35</sup> he said, "I will hear your case when your accusers get here." Then he ordered that Paul be kept under guard in Herod's palace.

*1. Why did the Romans send such a large detachment to guard Paul on his journey to Caesarea?*

*2. How is the commander's letter different from the facts of the events as told by Luke?*

*3. How is God using the power of Rome to advance his cause through Paul? How might God do similar things today?*

## DAY FIVE READING AND QUESTIONS

Reread the entire passage (Acts 22:30-23:35)

*1. What advantages of Roman citizenship does Paul enjoy in this story?*

*2. Why would Paul not know that Ananias was high priest?*

*3. In your own life's story, can you remember a time of great difficulty that only later you came to understand was part of God's working in a mighty way? Share the story.*

## MEDITATION

Paul confidently looked in the eyes of his accusers and defended the integrity of his actions. He then proposed he was under attack because of his belief in the resurrection. Did he say this knowing it would incite a riot? Remember, Paul was not concerned about his own well-being. He was not trying to escape. Long before, he had fully entrusted his life to the Lord. It is most likely that Paul brought up the resurrection because he still hoped that the Pharisees at least would hear him out. After all, many had already turned to Jesus.

The Lord's appearance to Paul that night was a wonderful manifestation of grace. In all the wrongful behavior demonstrated against Paul, in all the confusion and chaos, God was at work. Paul was faithful, and God had plans. Paul would proclaim the gospel in Rome itself. And all along the way there would be those who would listen and turn their hearts to God. Whenever we are about God's work, he will produce good fruit even when we cannot see it. What looks disastrous to us may be a great victory. This is the way of the cross. While the story seems to keep getting worse, no one can short circuit God's plan. God used Paul's nephew to spoil the scheme of those who had planned to ambush Paul and kill him. Have you ever wondered what happened to those foolish men who vowed they would not eat nor drink until they had killed Paul? It is wonderfully assuring once again to see that no individual or group can defeat the ultimate purposes of God.

Paul arrived safely at Caesarea under God's protection. Now how would God provide safe conduct to Rome for Paul? As difficult as the journey would be, as long as the journey will take, God was at work at every turn. Every time Paul told his story of conversion, people are listening—and while it may seem that little was being done, seeds of the kingdom were being planted all along the way. From Paul we learn the role of the faithful, unquestioning servant. The focus, the very purpose of his life, was to be faithful to God's calling. Do we have a sense of God's purpose for our lives? Do we listen for his voice? Do we choose to live under his protection?

"Lord, help me to see the purpose of my life in your plan. Teach me to trust in you and you alone."

# FELIX HEARS THE STORY

## (ACTS 24)

## DAY ONE READING AND QUESTIONS

[1] Five days later the high priest Ananias went down to Caesarea with some of the elders and a lawyer named Tertullus, and they brought their charges against Paul before the governor. [2] When Paul was called in, Tertullus presented his case before Felix: "We have enjoyed a long period of peace under you, and your foresight has brought about reforms in this nation. [3] Everywhere and in every way, most excellent Felix, we acknowledge this with profound gratitude. [4] But in order not to weary you further, I would request that you be kind enough to hear us briefly. [5] "We have found this man to be a troublemaker, stirring up riots among the Jews all over the world. He is a ringleader of the Nazarene sect [6] and even tried to desecrate the temple; so we seized him. [7][8] By examining him yourself you will be able to learn the truth about all these charges we are bringing against him." [9] The Jews joined in the accusation, asserting that these things were true.

*1. Do you think Tertullus' opening statement to Felix was sincere? Why or why not?*

*2. What was Tertullus' primary accusation against Paul?*

*3. What was the basis of the charge that Paul attempted to desecrate the temple?*

## DAY TWO READING AND QUESTIONS

[10] When the governor motioned for him to speak, Paul replied: "I know that for a number of years you have been a judge over this nation; so I gladly make my defense. [11] You can easily verify that no more than twelve days ago I went up to Jerusalem to worship. [12] My accusers did not find me arguing with anyone at the temple, or stirring up a crowd in the synagogues or anywhere else in the city. [13] And they cannot prove to you the charges they are now making against me. [14] However, I admit that I worship the God of our fathers as a follower of the Way, which they call a sect. I believe everything that agrees with the Law and that is written in the Prophets, [15] and I have the same hope in God as these men, that there will be a resurrection of both the righteous and the wicked.

*1. What was Paul's purpose for being at the temple, according to his own words?*

*2. What did Paul admit? What does his admission show about his view of the relationship between the worship of God and being a follower of the Way?*

*3. Why do you think Paul began by expressing his common belief with his accusers?*

## DAY THREE READING AND QUESTIONS

[16] So I strive always to keep my conscience clear before God and man. [17] "After an absence of several years, I came to Jerusalem to bring my people gifts for the poor and to present offerings. [18] I was ceremonially clean when they found me in the temple courts doing this. There was no crowd with me, nor was I involved in any disturbance. [19] But there are some Jews from the province of Asia, who ought to be here before you and bring charges if they have anything against me. [20] Or these who are here should state what crime they found in me when I stood before the Sanhedrin— [21] unless it was this one thing I shouted as I stood in their presence: 'It is concerning the resurrection of the dead that I am on trial before you today.'"

1. *What was Paul's purpose in coming to Jerusalem, according to these verses?*

2. *Why did Paul bring up the subject of the Jews from the province of Asia?*

3. *Why did Paul demand they bring forward charges from his previous meeting with the Sanhedrin? What can we learn from Paul's behavior in all this?*

## DAY FOUR READING AND QUESTIONS

[22] Then Felix, who was well acquainted with the Way, adjourned the proceedings. "When Lysias the commander comes," he said, "I will decide your case." [23] He ordered the centurion to keep Paul under guard but to give him some freedom and permit his friends to take

care of his needs. ²⁴ Several days later Felix came with his wife Drusilla, who was a Jewess. He sent for Paul and listened to him as he spoke about faith in Christ Jesus. ²⁵ As Paul discoursed on righteousness, self-control and the judgment to come, Felix was afraid and said, "That's enough for now! You may leave. When I find it convenient, I will send for you." ²⁶ At the same time he was hoping that Paul would offer him a bribe, so he sent for him frequently and talked with him. ²⁷ When two years had passed, Felix was succeeded by Porcius Festus, but because Felix wanted to grant a favor to the Jews, he left Paul in prison.

*1. How do you think Felix was "well acquainted" with the Way?*

*2. Why do you think Felix and his wife sent for Paul?*

*3. What was the content of Paul's discussion with Felix? Why do you think this caused Felix to fear?*

## DAY FIVE READING AND QUESTIONS

Reread the entire passage (Acts 24:1-27)

*1. What surprises you most about Paul's dealings with Felix?*

*2. What do you think Paul was thinking during those two years of detainment?*

*3. Have you had experiences in your life when you felt God was distant and uncaring, only later to see his marvelous plan in what you had suffered? If so, discuss this.*

# MEDITATION

Paul acknowledged the power of Felix to judge and his reputation for fairness, and then presented a very straightforward and simple defense. He explained that he went to the temple to worship, to take offerings for the poor—and took no part in stirring up the crowd. Paul wanted to make sure all knew, however, that he was indeed a follower of Jesus, a believer in "the Way." Here he made a careful distinction: he said "they" (his accusers) call "the Way" a sect. Paul clarified that "the Way" was not a sect, but the very essence of the Law fulfilled. He was convinced that all the Law and the Prophets pointed to Jesus.

Who could doubt Paul's sincerity and allegiance to God's law? In that first hearing Felix could find nothing wrong with what Paul had done. While he waited for the Jewish leaders to arrive with their accusations against Paul, Felix, along with his wife, invited Paul to speak to them. What did he speak about? He spoke of faith in Christ Jesus, righteousness, self-control, and the judgment to come. You can be sure that Paul called Felix to repent and turn to Jesus, where he, too, could find life. Paul did not waver, though he was held for over two years. He knew God was sending him to Rome.

Have you ever had to wait for something without understanding what was happening? Can you imagine, like Paul, waiting for two long years for God's next move? Do we have the faith to believe that God is working in all the circumstances of our lives? I have known those who have nearly lost their faith because God did not give them what they felt they needed when they wanted it. The great people of faith in the Scriptures were willing to wait on the Lord and trust him to accomplish his will even in the seemingly fruitless years of waiting. What of the prophets, who spoke of the great blessing to come (1 Peter 1:10-12), but never saw those blessings? They faithfully spoke the word of

God knowing they would not experience its fulfillment. We, instead, have seen the "yes" of all of God's promises (2 Corinthians 1:20)—Jesus Christ has come. All of God's promises will be fulfilled, but on His timetable, not ours. Do we have the faith to wait?

"Lord, teach me to wait on you."

# PAUL BEFORE FESTUS
## (ACTS 25)

### DAY ONE READING AND QUESTIONS

[1] Three days after arriving in the province, Festus went up from Caesarea to Jerusalem, [2] where the chief priests and Jewish leaders appeared before him and presented the charges against Paul. [3] They urgently requested Festus, as a favor to them, to have Paul transferred to Jerusalem, for they were preparing an ambush to kill him along the way. [4] Festus answered, "Paul is being held at Caesarea, and I myself am going there soon. [5] Let some of your leaders come with me and press charges against the man there, if he has done anything wrong." [6] After spending eight or ten days with them, he went down to Caesarea, and the next day he convened the court and ordered that Paul be brought before him. [7] When Paul appeared, the Jews who had come down from Jerusalem stood around him, bringing many serious charges against him, which they could not prove.

*1. Even after two years, what was the first thing on the Jewish leaders' minds when they met their new governor?*

*2. Do you think Festus knew of the Jewish leaders' previous attempts to kill Paul?*

*3. Why were those opposed to Paul still unable to construct a strong case against him?*

## DAY TWO READING AND QUESTIONS

[8] Then Paul made his defense: "I have done nothing wrong against the law of the Jews or against the temple or against Caesar." [9] Festus, wishing to do the Jews a favor, said to Paul, "Are you willing to go up to Jerusalem and stand trial before me there on these charges?" [10] Paul answered: "I am now standing before Caesar's court, where I ought to be tried. I have not done any wrong to the Jews, as you yourself know very well. [11] If, however, I am guilty of doing anything deserving death, I do not refuse to die. But if the charges brought against me by these Jews are not true, no one has the right to hand me over to them. I appeal to Caesar!" [12] After Festus had conferred with his council, he declared: "You have appealed to Caesar. To Caesar you will go!"

*1. Why did Festus want to do a favor for the Jews?*

*2. Why did Paul refuse to return to Jerusalem?*

*3. Was Paul afraid to die? Why is this important in his defense? Are you afraid to die?*

## DAY THREE READING AND QUESTIONS

[13] A few days later King Agrippa and Bernice arrived at Caesarea to pay their respects to Festus. [14] Since they were spending many days there, Festus discussed Paul's case with the king. He said: "There is a man here whom Felix left as a prisoner. [15] When I went to Jerusalem, the chief priests and elders of the Jews brought charges against him and asked that he be condemned. [16] "I told them that it is not the Roman custom to hand over any man before he has faced his accusers and has had an opportunity to defend himself against their charges. [17] When they came here with me, I did not delay the case, but convened the court the next day and ordered the man to be brought in. [18] When his accusers got up to speak, they did not charge him with any of the crimes I had expected. [19] Instead, they had some points of dispute with him about their own religion and about a dead man named Jesus who Paul claimed was alive. [20] I was at a loss how to investigate such matters; so I asked if he would be willing to go to Jerusalem and stand trial there on these charges. [21] When Paul made his appeal to be held over for the Emperor's decision, I ordered him held until I could send him to Caesar." [22] Then Agrippa said to Festus, "I would like to hear this man myself." He replied, "Tomorrow you will hear him."

   *1. Why do you think Festus brought up the case of Paul before King Agrippa?*

   *2. What crimes do you think Festus expected the Jews to bring against Paul?*

   *3. Why do you think Agrippa wanted to hear Paul's case himself?*

## DAY FOUR READING AND QUESTIONS

[23] The next day Agrippa and Bernice came with great pomp and entered the audience room with the high ranking officers and the leading men of the city. At the command of Festus, Paul was brought in. [24] Festus said: "King Agrippa, and all who are present with us, you see this man! The whole Jewish community has petitioned me about him in Jerusalem and here in Caesarea, shouting that he ought not to live any longer. [25] I found he had done nothing deserving of death, but because he made his appeal to the Emperor I decided to send him to Rome. [26] But I have nothing definite to write to His Majesty about him. Therefore I have brought him before all of you, and especially before you, King Agrippa, so that as a result of this investigation I may have something to write. [27] For I think it is unreasonable to send on a prisoner without specifying the charges against him."

*1. Why does Luke mention the great pomp surrounding this event?*

*2. What had Festus not found in researching Paul's case?*

*3. What is Festus seeking through this formal hearing?*

## DAY FIVE READING AND QUESTIONS

Reread the entire passage (Acts 25:1-27)

*1. What does Luke see as Rome's role in this story?*

*2. What do you think Luke wants his original readers to understand about the power of Rome and the power of God?*

*3. Do you think God works in similar ways today? How might God use present world powers to help spread the Good News?*

# MEDITATION

Even taking into account all the power and pomp of the Roman Empire, Luke wants to make sure we understand who is in control. God is again using a pagan power to achieve his purposes. Those opposed to Paul simply cannot make a case against him. But why should this matter? Jesus himself was wrongly accused, and the Romans did not stand on his behalf. Pilate was not about to stand against the will of the people, even though he knew Jesus was innocent. He allowed Jesus to be crucified. Why, then, not let Paul die? Was it because he was a Roman citizen that the Romans protected him and not Jesus?

Not according to Luke's thinking—the only difference between Paul and Jesus was what God was doing through them. It was God's will that Jesus die for our salvation. Likewise, it is God's will that Paul live, in order for him to preach the gospel in Rome. What Jesus did in Luke, the church and faithful believers do in Acts. Sometimes, as in the case of Stephen and James, the story of a believer's life on this earth ends in death. Other times, God allows one to escape imprisonment. At other times, the imprisonment itself is God's protection. Luke's point is this: all is subject to the power and will of God.

As one reads Luke's account of the entry processional preceding Paul's hearing, one cannot help but sense the amusing irony. These individuals were secure and proud in their power and might. These were the leading citizens of Caesarea, the Roman governor, and even the king and his wife—all should be awed by their status in life. But the one who was really in control was in chains. Why? Because God was with him.

When we stand with God, who can stand against us?

"Lord, thank you for always being with us. We know we can stand against all things if we are standing with you."

# AGRIPPA HEARS THE STORY
## (ACTS 26)

## DAY ONE READING AND QUESTIONS

¹ Then Agrippa said to Paul, "You have permission to speak for yourself." So Paul motioned with his hand and began his defense: ² "King Agrippa, I consider myself fortunate to stand before you today as I make my defense against all the accusations of the Jews, ³ and especially so because you are well acquainted with all the Jewish customs and controversies. Therefore, I beg you to listen to me patiently. ⁴ "The Jews all know the way I have lived ever since I was a child, from the beginning of my life in my own country, and also in Jerusalem. ⁵ They have known me for a long time and can testify, if they are willing, that according to the strictest sect of our religion, I lived as a Pharisee. ⁶And now it is because of my hope in what God has promised our fathers that I am on trial today. ⁷ This is the promise our twelve tribes are hoping to see fulfilled as they earnestly serve God day and night. O king, it is because of this hope that the Jews are accusing me. ⁸ Why should any of you consider it incredible that God raises the dead? ⁹ "I too was convinced that I ought to do all that was

possible to oppose the name of Jesus of Nazareth. [10] And that is just what I did in Jerusalem. On the authority of the chief priests I put many of the saints in prison, and when they were put to death, I cast my vote against them. [11] Many a time I went from one synagogue to another to have them punished, and I tried to force them to blaspheme. In my obsession against them, I even went to foreign cities to persecute them.

*1. Why did Paul consider himself fortunate to stand before Agrippa?*

*2. How well were the Jews acquainted with Paul's life, according to him?*

*3. Why was Paul, in his own words, originally against the name of Jesus?*

## DAY TWO READING AND QUESTIONS

[12] "On one of these journeys I was going to Damascus with the authority and commission of the chief priests. [13] About noon, O king, as I was on the road, I saw a light from heaven, brighter than the sun, blazing around me and my companions. [14] We all fell to the ground, and I heard a voice saying to me in Aramaic, 'Saul, Saul, why do you persecute me? It is hard for you to kick against the goads.' [15] "Then I asked, 'Who are you, Lord?' "'I am Jesus, whom you are persecuting,' the Lord replied. [16] 'Now get up and stand on your feet. I have appeared to you to appoint you as a servant and as a witness of what you have seen of me and what I will show you. [17] I will rescue you from your own people and from the Gentiles. I am sending you to them [18] to open their eyes and turn them from darkness to light, and from the power of Satan to God, so that they may receive forgiveness of sins and a place among those who are sanctified by faith in me.' [19] "So then, King

Agrippa, I was not disobedient to the vision from heaven. [20]First to those in Damascus, then to those in Jerusalem and in all Judea, and to the Gentiles also, I preached that they should repent and turn to God and prove their repentance by their deeds. [21] That is why the Jews seized me in the temple courts and tried to kill me. [22] But I have had God's help to this very day, and so I stand here and testify to small and great alike. I am saying nothing beyond what the prophets and Moses said would happen— [23] that the Christ would suffer and, as the first to rise from the dead, would proclaim light to his own people and to the Gentiles."

1. *Why do you think Paul mentions the voice speaking to him in Aramaic?*

2. *What was Paul's mission, according to his vision?*

3. *How does Paul summarize his message to all with whom he spoke? How would you summarize your story?*

## DAY THREE READING AND QUESTIONS

[24] At this point Festus interrupted Paul's defense. "You are out of your mind, Paul!" he shouted. "Your great learning is driving you insane." [25] "I am not insane, most excellent Festus," Paul replied. "What I am saying is true and reasonable. [26] The king is familiar with these things, and I can speak freely to him. I am convinced that none of this has escaped his notice, because it was not done in a corner. [27] King Agrippa, do you believe the prophets? I know you do."

1. *Why did Festus think Paul was out of his mind?*

2. *What does his phrase, "Your great learning," tell us about Festus' view of Paul?*

3. *What does Paul's comment about all this "not happening in a corner" mean?*

## DAY FOUR READING AND QUESTIONS

[28] Then Agrippa said to Paul, "Do you think that in such a short time you can persuade me to be a Christian?" [29] Paul replied, "Short time or long— I pray God that not only you but all who are listening to me today may become what I am, except for these chains." [30] The king rose, and with him the governor and Bernice and those sitting with them. [31] They left the room, and while talking with one another, they said, "This man is not doing anything that deserves death or imprisonment." [32] Agrippa said to Festus, "This man could have been set free if he had not appealed to Caesar."

1. *What did Agrippa realize about what Paul was actually trying to do?*

2. *What does Paul's response tell us about what he thinks of life in Jesus?*

3. *Could you say the same thing that Paul says about his life in Jesus (excluding, of course, his comment about his chains)? Why or why not?*

## DAY FIVE READING AND QUESTIONS

Reread the entire passage (Acts 26:1-32)

1. *What do you find most compelling in this chapter?*

*2. If you were put on trial to defend your faith, what would you say?*

*3. What was the ultimate judgment of this hearing? Why is this important to the story?*

# MEDITATION

Luke describes Paul's hearing before Agrippa as an official occasion, with proper pageantry being shown to the king and his wife. What a great opportunity to preach the gospel! Festus begins the proceedings by stating the official reason for the hearing—he needed formal charges to accompany Paul to Rome. Agrippa was known for his understanding of Jewish customs. Perhaps he could articulate a charge against Paul for his ultimate hearing before Caesar.

Paul once again presented his story. As he spoke of the resurrection, Festus interrupted him. Festus had no point of reference by which to understand what Paul was saying. How could this be? A dead Savior, a risen Lord? A Jew killed by the Romans somehow able to save both Jew and Roman? It is interesting that Festus attributed Paul's "madness" to his great learning. It was obvious to Festus that Paul was not a raving lunatic, but intelligent and articulate.

Paul's response to Festus is fascinating. He states that Festus is not properly prepared to hear the message, for it is both reasonable and true. Agrippa, however, schooled in what the prophets had taught, was able to grasp what Paul was saying. Paul based his defense on Agrippa's understanding of the prophets. Agrippa had indeed been listening.

The intended meaning of Agrippa's response to Paul will be debated as long as time exists. Was Agrippa "almost persuaded"? Or was he taunting Paul, making fun of Paul's attempt to persuade him? I think Agrippa was surprised. It was at this point that Agrippa realized

Paul was not making a defense for himself at all. Instead, he was attempting to convince all present that Jesus of Nazareth was indeed the Christ. Agrippa, in sudden realization of what Paul was doing, was asking with disbelief, "Are you trying to convert me in such a short time? Shouldn't you be trying to defend yourself instead?" Paul's answer is one of the great highlights of Luke's work. Paul said, "King Agrippa, whether I have a few moments with you or a long time, all I want is for you to know and experience the life I have found—what I really want is for everyone here, whether a person of great importance or the lowliest servant, to find life in Jesus as I have. I wish you could all be like me—except of course (envision Paul lifting his chains for all to see and even smiling as he continues) for these chains." Laughter? Maybe. Astounding effect? What do you think?

Those of us who live in places where we are free to proclaim our faith ought to be deeply convicted to use every opportunity to speak of life in Jesus. It is a life of such hope, such deep meaning, such joy, and such purpose that we should want everyone we know to find life in Jesus. Maybe we have a deep sorrow in our lives. Maybe we carry a difficult burden. But that does not change the deep assurance we have in Jesus. We still ought to be able to say with Paul, "The only thing I know is, except for this burden that I bear, I want more than anything else for others to know Jesus as I do."

"Lord, help me speak often of your amazing love. May I understand the joy of walking with you to the extent that I want everyone to have a relationship with you."

# A DANGEROUS JOURNEY AT SEA

## (ACTS 27:1-28:10)

### DAY ONE READING AND QUESTIONS

[1] When it was decided that we would sail for Italy, Paul and some other prisoners were handed over to a centurion named Julius, who belonged to the Imperial Regiment. [2] We boarded a ship from Adramyttium about to sail for ports along the coast of the province of Asia, and we put out to sea. Aristarchus, a Macedonian from Thessalonica, was with us. [3] The next day we landed at Sidon; and Julius, in kindness to Paul, allowed him to go to his friends so they might provide for his needs. [4] From there we put out to sea again and passed to the lee of Cyprus because the winds were against us. [5] When we had sailed across the open sea off the coast of Cilicia and Pamphylia, we landed at Myra in Lycia. [6] There the centurion found an Alexandrian ship sailing for Italy and put us on board. [7] We made slow headway for many days and had difficulty arriving off Cnidus. When the wind did not allow us to hold our course, we sailed to the lee of Crete, opposite Salmone. [8] We moved along the coast with difficulty and came to a place called Fair Havens, near the town of Lasea. [9]Much time had been lost, and sailing had already become dangerous because by now it was after the Fast. So Paul warned them, [10] "Men, I

can see that our voyage is going to be disastrous and bring great loss to ship and cargo, and to our own lives also." [11] But the centurion, instead of listening to what Paul said, followed the advice of the pilot and of the owner of the ship. [12] Since the harbor was unsuitable to winter in, the majority decided that we should sail on, hoping to reach Phoenix and winter there. This was a harbor in Crete, facing both southwest and northwest. [13] When a gentle south wind began to blow, they thought they had obtained what they wanted; so they weighed anchor and sailed along the shore of Crete.

> *1. Why do you think Paul warned the centurion of the danger that awaited them?*

> *2. Why do you think the pilot and owner of the ship felt they should sail on?*

> *3. Have you ever been in a storm at sea or known someone who was? If so, recall or relate the experience.*

## DAY TWO READING AND QUESTIONS

[14] Before very long, a wind of hurricane force, called the "northeaster," swept down from the island. [15] The ship was caught by the storm and could not head into the wind; so we gave way to it and were driven along. [16] As we passed to the lee of a small island called Cauda, we were hardly able to make the lifeboat secure. [17] When the men had hoisted it aboard, they passed ropes under the ship itself to hold it together. Fearing that they would run aground on the sandbars of Syrtis, they lowered the sea anchor and let the ship be driven along. [18] We took such a violent battering from the storm that the next day they began to throw the cargo overboard. [19] On the third day, they

threw the ship's tackle overboard with their own hands. [20] When neither sun nor stars appeared for many days and the storm continued raging, we finally gave up all hope of being saved. [21] After the men had gone a long time without food, Paul stood up before them and said: "Men, you should have taken my advice not to sail from Crete; then you would have spared yourselves this damage and loss. [22] But now I urge you to keep up your courage, because not one of you will be lost; only the ship will be destroyed. [23] Last night an angel of the God whose I am and whom I serve stood beside me [24] and said, 'Do not be afraid, Paul. You must stand trial before Caesar; and God has graciously given you the lives of all who sail with you.' [25] So keep up your courage, men, for I have faith in God that it will happen just as he told me. [26] Nevertheless, we must run aground on some island."

*1. Why would the crew begin to throw cargo overboard?*

*2. What was Luke's thinking during the storm?*

*3. Why did Paul remind them of his warning not to sail?*

## DAY THREE READING AND QUESTIONS

[27] On the fourteenth night we were still being driven across the Adriatic Sea, when about midnight the sailors sensed they were approaching land. [28] They took soundings and found that the water was a hundred and twenty feet deep. A short time later they took soundings again and found it was ninety feet deep. [29] Fearing that we would be dashed against the rocks, they dropped four anchors from the stern and prayed for daylight. [30] In an attempt to escape from the ship, the sailors let the lifeboat down into the sea, pretending they were going to lower some anchors from the bow. [31] Then Paul said to

the centurion and the soldiers, "Unless these men stay with the ship, you cannot be saved." [32] So the soldiers cut the ropes that held the lifeboat and let it fall away. [33] Just before dawn Paul urged them all to eat. "For the last fourteen days," he said, "you have been in constant suspense and have gone without food—you haven't eaten anything. [34] Now I urge you to take some food. You need it to survive. Not one of you will lose a single hair from his head." [35] After he said this, he took some bread and gave thanks to God in front of them all. Then he broke it and began to eat. [36] They were all encouraged and ate some food themselves. [37] Altogether there were 276 of us on board. [38] When they had eaten as much as they wanted, they lightened the ship by throwing the grain into the sea. [39] When daylight came, they did not recognize the land, but they saw a bay with a sandy beach, where they decided to run the ship aground if they could. [40] Cutting loose the anchors, they left them in the sea and at the same time untied the ropes that held the rudders. Then they hoisted the foresail to the wind and made for the beach. [41] But the ship struck a sandbar and ran aground. The bow stuck fast and would not move, and the stern was broken to pieces by the pounding of the surf. [42] The soldiers planned to kill the prisoners to prevent any of them from swimming away and escaping. [43] But the centurion wanted to spare Paul's life and kept them from carrying out their plan. He ordered those who could swim to jump overboard first and get to land. [44] The rest were to get there on planks or on pieces of the ship. In this way everyone reached land in safety.

1. *How do you think the sailors were able to sense they were nearing land?*

2. *Are you surprised by the number of men who were on the ship?*

3. *How was Paul able to convince the men to eat after such a perilous time at sea? Why was Paul not afraid?*

## DAY FOUR READING AND QUESTIONS

[1] Once safely on shore, we found out that the island was called Malta. [2] The islanders showed us unusual kindness. They built a fire and welcomed us all because it was raining and cold. [3] Paul gathered a pile of brushwood and, as he put it on the fire, a viper, driven out by the heat, fastened itself on his hand. [4] When the islanders saw the snake hanging from his hand, they said to each other, "This man must be a murderer; for though he escaped from the sea, Justice has not allowed him to live." [5] But Paul shook the snake off into the fire and suffered no ill effects. [6] The people expected him to swell up or suddenly fall dead, but after waiting a long time and seeing nothing unusual happen to him, they changed their minds and said he was a god. [7] There was an estate nearby that belonged to Publius, the chief official of the island. He welcomed us to his home and for three days entertained us hospitably. [8] His father was sick in bed, suffering from fever and dysentery. Paul went in to see him and, after prayer, placed his hands on him and healed him. [9] When this had happened, the rest of the sick on the island came and were cured. [10] They honored us in many ways and when we were ready to sail, they furnished us with the supplies we needed.

*1. Why did the islanders think Paul was a murderer?*

*2. Why did they change their minds and think he was a god?*

*3. Why were the islanders so kind and generous with Paul and those with him?*

## DAY FIVE READING AND QUESTIONS

Reread the entire passage (Acts 27:1-28:10)

1. *How was Paul able to remain calm in the midst of the terrible storm? What can we learn from this?*

2. *How was Paul able to remain so focused on the needs of others? Can we do this?*

3. *What do you think Paul talked about during the months he spent on Malta?*

# MEDITATION

Shipwrecks were common occurrences, especially for those who were foolish enough to sail in the late fall and early winter. This is exactly what happened to Paul. A hurricane force wind arose and nothing could be done. It quickly became a sheer battle for survival. In the midst of the terrifying storm, one person was at peace. Even Luke was terrified after days and days of the relentless storm. He gave up all hope of ever seeing land again. Paul was at peace because knew that what he had entrusted to God was not at risk.

Paul's work on the island of Malta is a wonderful story. The islanders were warm and helpful. They did not know what to think of Paul. He was bitten by a poisonous snake, but nothing happened to him. Before long, he was in the home of leader of the island, healing the sick in the powerful name of Jesus. Today a statue of Paul stands on a sandy beach on Malta. What a thrill to walk that beach and think about the giant of faith who once, out of concern for others, in the midst of a driving rain storm, after enduring the terrors of a storm at sea for over two weeks, went about gathering firewood to warm the sick, weary, and cold.

Jesus invites us to this life, a life of unwavering faith in God unlike any other experience offered on this earth. It is terrifying to give complete control of your life to God. Shipwrecks sometimes seem to be the normative experience in this life of faith. But the greater terror is to refuse to give God that which only he can keep safely in his hands. It might be a wild ride, but with God in control, there is no reason to fear.

"Father, help us see each event in our lives as an opportunity to glorify you. In the midst of the storms of life, give us a spirit of calm so that we might serve others in your name."

# PAUL IN ROME

## (ACTS 28:11-31)

### DAY ONE READING AND QUESTIONS

[11] After three months we put out to sea in a ship that had wintered in the island. It was an Alexandrian ship with the figurehead of the twin gods Castor and Pollux. [12] We put in at Syracuse and stayed there three days. [13] From there we set sail and arrived at Rhegium. The next day the south wind came up, and on the following day we reached Puteoli. [14] There we found some brothers who invited us to spend a week with them. And so we came to Rome. [15] The brothers there had heard that we were coming, and they traveled as far as the Forum of

Appius and the Three Taverns to meet us. At the sight of these men Paul thanked God and was encouraged. [16] When we got to Rome, Paul was allowed to live by himself, with a soldier to guard him.

*1. What does Paul's freedom to travel demonstrate?*

*2. Why do you think Paul was so encouraged by the brethren from Rome?*

*3. What do Paul's living arrangements show about the Roman's trust of Paul?*

## DAY TWO READING AND QUESTIONS

[17] Three days later he called together the leaders of the Jews. When they had assembled, Paul said to them: "My brothers, although I have done nothing against our people or against the customs of our ancestors, I was arrested in Jerusalem and handed over to the Romans. [18] They examined me and wanted to release me, because I was not guilty of any crime deserving death. [19] But when the Jews objected, I was com-pelled to appeal to Caesar—not that I had any charge to bring against my own people. [20] For this reason I have asked to see you and talk with you. It is because of the hope of Israel that I am bound with this chain."

*1. Why do you think Paul began his work in Rome by talking to the Jewish leaders?*

*2. What does Paul's first statement to the Jewish leaders show?*

*3. In what sense was Paul imprisoned because of "the hope of Israel"?*

## DAY THREE READING AND QUESTIONS

[21] They replied, "We have not received any letters from Judea concerning you, and none of the brothers who have come from there has reported or said anything bad about you. [22] But we want to hear what your views are, for we know that people everywhere are talking against this sect." [23] They arranged to meet Paul on a certain day, and came in even larger numbers to the place where he was staying. From morning till evening he explained and declared to them the kingdom of God and tried to convince them about Jesus from the Law of Moses and from the Prophets.

> *1. Why do you think the Jewish leaders of Rome had not heard anything about Paul?*
>
> *2. About what did the leaders want to know?*
>
> *3. What was the content of Paul's message to the Jewish leaders?*

## DAY FOUR READING AND QUESTIONS

[24] Some were convinced by what he said, but others would not believe. [25] They disagreed among themselves and began to leave after Paul had made this final statement: "The Holy Spirit spoke the truth to your forefathers when he said through Isaiah the prophet: [26] "'Go to this people and say, "You will be ever hearing but never undestanding; you will be ever seeing but never perceiving." [27] For this people's heart has become calloused; they hardly hear with their ears, and they have closed their eyes. Otherwise they might see with their eyes, hear with their ears, understand with their hearts and turn, and I would heal

them.' [28] "Therefore I want you to know that God's salvation has been sent to the Gentiles, and they will listen!" [29] [30] For two whole years Paul stayed there in his own rented house and welcomed all who came to see him. [31] Boldly and without hindrance he preached the kingdom of God and taught about the Lord Jesus Christ.

1. *What was the response of those who heard Paul speak? How does this compare to other times when Paul preached?*

2. *Why would Paul quote the verse about people not accepting God's word?*

3. *What is God's ultimate desire for his word?*

## DAY FIVE READING AND QUESTIONS

Reread the entire passage (Acts 28:11-31)

1. *What do you think is the most important teaching in this final episode in Acts?*

2. *If you were in Paul's place, what would you have said to the Jewish leaders?*

3. *What is your response to the ending of Acts? Do you hear the call to join in the story? Why or why not?*

# MEDITATION

We have come to the end of Luke's marvelous work. Jesus is indeed alive in his church. Can you imagine how much Paul was encouraged by those who joined him on the walk to Rome? At every point of the journey, believers are waiting to join us on our "Appian Way" as we walk through this life. We are never alone as we work to expand God's reign on earth.

In this final episode, Paul defends himself one more time. As we have come to expect, some were open to his words and others were not. Luke chooses his words carefully here. Those who did not believe intentionally chose the path of unbelief. They refused to believe. There was no confusion, no desire to hear more, just intentional rejection. The cost of placing their faith in Jesus was too high.

Paul ended his presentation with a verse that confounds many: Isaiah 6:10. How is it that God wants his word preached to ears that will not hear and hearts that will not change? The point is—the word of God is indeed powerful and true. However, it is humanity's responsibility to accept it and allow it to change them. What is the purpose of God's revelation? It is to give sight, to allow people to hear the truth, and to heal their broken lives. What we see throughout Luke and Acts is that those who were willing to see and hear received their sight and were healed. Unbelievably, there were many who refused to be healed. They chose to remain blind.

As Luke's telling of the story ends, Paul continues his work without hindrance—explaining and giving evidence that Jesus was indeed the Messiah. He proclaims that because of Jesus' great sacrifice, we can repent, be cleansed of our sins, and walk deeply into the kingdom of God. Are we listening?

Why does the story come to such an abrupt end? I suggested in the introduction that this is Luke's way of inviting us into God's story.

The spread of the gospel does not end in Rome. It would not end with Paul's death. This story is not about Paul; it is about Jesus alive in his church, about God's work through Jesus and the Holy Spirit continuing through his faithful servants. What Jesus did in Luke's gospel through the guidance of the Holy Spirit, the church does in Acts. Now we are the ones who stand at center stage. God lovingly invites us through Luke to participate in "the Way." We pick up the baton from Paul and carry it on in our own lives.

Has every person had the chance to hear the story of Jesus the Christ? There will be those who refuse to obey, but there are those who will obey given the chance to hear. Will we continue the bold proclamation of the good news of God's kingdom? Will we shout to the nations that we have found abundant life in Christ Jesus? Will we dedicate our lives to calling all to join us in God's kingdom?

"Dear Lord, thank you for the marvelous story of Jesus alive in his church. Thank you for the wonderful examples of faith as our brothers and sisters submitted their lives to you. May we open our hearts to receive your call to participate in the coming of your kingdom throughout the world. Father, may Jesus continue to be alive in his church."